BUSINESS ETIQUETTE

DEVELOPING YOUR REPUTATION OF PROFESSIONALISM WITH BUSINESS ETIQUETTE

Joe is a friendly employee and popular among his coworkers. He works efficiently and never gives his managers serious reason for concern. Although he's good at his job, he's unconsciously sabotaging his opportunities for advancement by not observing the norms for dressing professionally within his company. He dresses casually, although the office environment is conservative and a formal dress code requiring a jacket and tie is in place.

Professionalism refers to more than just doing your job well in isolation. It involves focusing on providing others with high-quality work and service, and on meeting or exceeding their expectations.

To do this, you have to be conscious of your surroundings and of how your actions impact others. You also have to consider the standards of professional behavior that apply in a given context, and respect these – not only through your actions, but in terms of the image you convey.

Although Joe might be highly skilled and efficient in the work he produces, his clothing choice is unprofessional because it doesn't meet his company's standards.

This course introduces you to the basics of business etiquette. It explains how to present yourself in the work environment by dressing professionally and maintaining a professional workspace. And it describes ways of protecting your professional reputation outside the office. This has become especially important in the era of the Internet and social media.

After completing this course, you'll be better equipped to practice good business etiquette. In turn, this can help you strengthen your professional reputation and build a successful career.

Developing Your Reputation with Business Etiquette
1. What is Business Etiquette?
2. Dressing Professionally
3. Maintaining a Professional Workspace
4. Professionalism Beyond the Office

WHAT IS BUSINESS ETIQUETTE?

After completing this topic, you should be able to identify the key characteristics of business etiquette

1. ETIQUETTE IN THE WORKPLACE

If you're under the impression that arriving for work in the right kind of suit makes you professional, you're mistaken. Sure, the way you dress and present yourself in your work environment is an important aspect of professionalism – but professionalism is a term that refers to more than just your wardrobe choice for the day.

Professionalism is something that's defined by certain standards or expectations.

What's considered to be professional in one workplace culture – or in one industry, organization, or division – may be considered completely unprofessional in another.

This is because your professionalism is judged on existing social norms for appropriate communication, image, competence, and demeanor in given contexts.

Being professional requires that you be mindful of your surroundings and of how your behavior may impact others. It involves considering others and being mannerly.

Select each aspect of professionalism to learn more about it.

Considering others

Being considerate of others involves simply considering how your words or actions affect others, and then adjusting your behavior accordingly.

For instance, a secretary works for two partners. One of the partners, who's under a lot of work pressure, sarcastically asks,

"Are you ever going to be done with that?" In this case, the partner should have considered the secretary's feelings – and the fact that the secretary might be under pressure to complete other work.

Being mannerly

Good manners are as important within working environments as they are outside of them. Saying "please" and "thank you" goes a long way, although there's more to it than that.

For example, a salesperson who keeps a client sitting in a waiting room while attending to a personal call isn't displaying very good manners.

Manners are just as important in today's fast-paced age as they ever were. Most individuals never mean to offend others, but bad manners can ruin work relationships and create unhealthy work environments.

To be professional and avoid damaging working relationships, you should endeavor to understand and respect others' needs.

You also need to meet their expectations about what constitutes appropriate behavior.

Business etiquette refers to the standards, or guidelines, that determine what constitutes good manners and professional behavior in the workplace.

The basic rules of business etiquette might not be spelled out explicitly, but they determine what the people around you expect and consider appropriate, given your position in an organization.

Say you often review business audio files as part of your work-related responsibilities, but others in the office find it quite distracting. To be professional, you'd be considerate and use headphones when listening to the audio files. This is good business etiquette because you're taking action to avoid offending or distracting those you work with. It shows you're aware of your actions and how they could affect people around you, and you're treating colleagues the way you'd expect them to treat you.

Business etiquette isn't static. It changes with the times, and can differ considerably between industries and in very different ways.

Seeeach factor for more information about differences in business etiquette.

With the times

Expectations about how businesspeople should dress and behave change with the times, as prevailing social norms and conditions change.

For example, it used to be considered much too familiar to use people's first names in business correspondence, unless you knew those people extremely well. But it's now fairly common practice to use people's first names after you've met them only once or twice.

Between industries

The industry individuals work in generally affects the ways they're expected to dress, speak, and behave.

For instance, lawyers are commonly expected to wear traditional business suits, whereas salespeople in a sports store would probably be expected to wear casual sports attire. Similarly, the lawyers and salespeople would be expected to interact with and respond to customers in quite different ways.

In different corporate cultures

The rules of business etiquette differ from one organization to another. For example, the corporate culture in one company might be conservative, with employees expected to dress and behave very formally – whereas in another organization, employees might be expected to look and act more casually.

Even within one organization, different departments may have slightly different cultures, which will affect the ways employees are expected to behave. For example, employees in a company's Finance Department may be expected to address clients very differently from the way employees in the Marketing Department are expected to.

2. THE EFFECTS OF POOR BUSINESS ETIQUETTE

Applying the rules of business etiquette in a manner appropriate to your position will enable you to present yourself in a polished, professional, and polite manner.

Over time, this can help you develop a good reputation and advance your career.

Follow along as Wendell, a marketing executive, meets with Lila, another executive at his company, to discuss an important project.

Lila: I'm glad we could meet to discuss the project plan today. We really need to get going on this.

Wendell: Yeah, especially since the deadline has been brought forward.

Lila: Let's start by discussing the project. Do you think it's realistic?

Wendell: Well…sorry, just hold on. I've just gotten a call from an old school friend of mine. We haven't seen each other in years!

Wendell is distracted by his cell phone.

Lila: OK…

Lila is surprised.

Wendell: Yeah, we just recently reconnected.

Wendell is still distracted by his phone.

Lila: I really don't think there's time for...

Lila is anxious.

Wendell: Just hold on.

Wendell is abrupt and distracted by his phone.

Lila: Wendell, we're actually in the middle of a meeting. It's rather rude of you to be chatting on your phone.

Lila is annoyed.

Reflect

Consider the meeting between Wendell and Lila.

What basic rule of business etiquette do you think Wendell violated?

Enter your response in the space provided and then select the Compare button for an answer.

Write down your response or enter it in a text file in your word-processor application (or in a text editor such as Notepad) and save it to your hard drive for later viewing and for comparison with the alternate opinion that follows.

Wendell's behavior

As you may have noted, business etiquette dictates that if you're in a meeting, you should give your full attention to the person or people in that meeting. You should switch off your cell phone so you don't disrupt the meeting and keep others waiting.

So, although Wendell may not have intended to be rude, his behavior was discourteous and unprofessional. Over time, this type of behavior could tarnish his reputation.

It's often the case that individuals compromise their business etiquette and manners for short-term productivity. They're under the misconception that good manners and business etiquette are niceties that can get in the way of being efficient. Instead of taking the time to say "please" or "thank you," for example, they may just shout out demands they think motivate people to act quickly.

This kind of behavior can harm your relationships with others at work. And over the long term, it may prevent you from receiving job promotions or even getting new jobs you apply for.

The business world is becoming increasingly competitive. Whether you move up in a company hierarchy or get a job you apply for no longer depends just on how qualified you are.

Your success will also depend on how you present yourself – including your manner with others and your appearance.

Poor business etiquette can have an impact on an entire organization. If executives or senior management lead by being rude, they're conveying the message that their conduct is acceptable – and other employees might follow suit. The result can be that treating others with disrespect becomes part of the organization's corporate culture. Ultimately, this can result in unhappy employees, high staff turnover, and a loss of customers.

Question

What are the key characteristics of business etiquette?

Options:

1. It helps you behave in a manner that's acceptable in the workplace

2. It consists of a universal set of rules for proper behavior that applies equally in all situations

3. It enables you to ensure your appearance is professional

4. It can contribute to employees' success in their jobs

5. It involves valuing politeness over efficiency in the workplace

6. It differs between industries

Answer

Option 1: This option is correct. Adhering to the rules of basic business etiquette helps ensure you behave and present yourself appropriately in a work environment.

Option 2: This is an incorrect option. The rules of business etiquette change with the times and differ both across industries and from one organization to another.

Option 3: This is a correct option. Business etiquette refers to guidelines, or norms, for behaving and presenting yourself in a professional manner in the workplace.

Option 4: This option is correct. Business etiquette determines the impression you make on others in the workplace and so can help determine how successful you are in your career.

Option 5: This option is incorrect. Adhering to the rules of basic business etiquette can help you to be more productive while still presenting yourself in a polished, professional, and polite manner.

Option 6: This is a correct option. Business etiquette changes over time, and can differ greatly across various industries and organizations.

3. SUMMARY

Business etiquette refers to the standards that determine what constitutes good manners and professional behavior in a work environment. It changes with the times, and differs across industries and in different organizations. Adhering to the rules of business etiquette that apply in your organization ensures you present yourself in a professional and polite way, and can enhance the success of your career.

DRESSING PROFESSIONALLY

After completing this topic, you should be able to determine whether an individual is dressed professionally in a given scenario

1. IMPORTANCE OF DRESSING PROFESSIONALLY

It may be true that you shouldn't judge a book by its cover – but it's equally true that the way you look affects what other people think about you and your level of professionalism. For example, suppose you meet with an investment broker because you're considering making a substantial investment. How would it make you feel if the broker were dressed in jeans and sandals, and had dirty fingernails? It's likely you'd feel better about the investment if the broker were more suitably dressed.

Question

Why do you think it's important to dress professionally?

Options:

1. You'll increase your confidence and feel better about yourself
2. You'll stand out from your colleagues and catch the boss's eye
3. You'll make a favorable impression
4. Both clients and colleagues will be more likely to try to befriend you on a personal level if it's clear you make an effort at work
5. People will be more likely to show you respect

Answer

Option 1: *This option is correct. Presenting a professional front will boost your self-confidence and self-esteem. You'll feel more capable, which will be reinforced when you get more positive reactions from others.*

Option 2: *This option is incorrect. Dressing professionally isn't about making a personal statement. You should dress to emphasize that you're a professional doing a job rather than trying to stand out.*

Option 3: *This is a correct option. You'll make a favorable impression if you dress well and look like the professional you are. This is because your appearance will send the message that you're competent and focused on your work.*

Option 4: *This option is incorrect. The way you dress for work should garner professional rather than personal respect.*

Option 5: *This option is correct. If you project a professional image, people are more likely to acknowledge your professional status and show you the corresponding respect.*

When they meet you face to face, people will judge your appearance. Before they've even heard a greeting, people have assigned you characteristics based on your looks. In business, people instill confidence in you if you look like a smart businessperson who takes care of your appearance.

Dressing professionally will also make you feel more capable, and boost your self-esteem and self-confidence in a business setting.

When considering dressing professionally, you have to ask yourself what message you send. The way you dress is a means of communicating with clients and colleagues.

Select each group to learn more about what your appearance conveys to them.

Clients

When you meet clients, the first impression you make is extremely important. You should try to convey a sense of professionalism through your appearance so clients know you're serious about your job and can be trusted to attend to their needs.

Colleagues

A professional appearance and adherence to your company's preferred dress code will let your colleagues know you're there to focus on work. Dressing in a way that draws attention may cause people to believe you're at work to get attention rather than do your job.

Your appearance should be consistent with your professional role. In other words, you should look the part. You'll inspire confidence in others, who'll be more likely to think you can handle your job well. It makes it more likely you'll command respect and can help you build your reputation and career.

Ideas about what constitutes professional dress differ from one industry and organization to another. They also differ based on the position you hold, and even based on the country or region you're in.

To fit in, you should determine what style of dress is acceptable in your organization and for people occupying your position.

For the remainder of this topic, you'll explore eight guidelines for dressing professionally, starting with the importance of abiding by your company's dress code.

2. ORGANIZATIONAL DRESS CODES

Although different types of dress are suitable in different scenarios, some general principles for dressing professionally do apply. The first of these is to abide by your organization's dress code – whether this is defined explicitly or implied from the way other employees dress.

Your clothes should be appropriate for your organization and suit your position. Different jobs within a single company require different attire. For example, you wouldn't expect a CEO to dress in the same way as someone who handles building maintenance.

If you examine different work environments, you'll notice different styles of dress. For example, consider how employees typically dress in a bank, an advertising agency, and a film production company.

See each type of organization to learn more about its typical dress code.

Bank

If you work in a formal business environment like a bank, you're generally expected to dress formally. When meeting with clients or serving customers, men usually wear conservative suits and ties, and women wear pantsuits or jackets with matching skirts.

Advertising agency

In an advertising agency, the relevant dress code might depend on the types of clients you typically serve or on the general image that the agency has chosen to portray.

For example, if an advertising agency deals with corporate clients like banks, employees may be expected to mirror the formal dress style of those clients. But if an advertising agency wants to project a trendy or more creative image, employees may wear fashionable designer clothes with a little more flair – including brand-name shirts, slacks, jeans, dresses, and jackets.

Film production company

Your position in a film production company would probably dictate what's your appropriate attire. As part of a film crew, for example, it might be acceptable to wear jeans, casual shirts, and even running shoes. But if you're responsible for negotiating financial backing with businesspeople, you'd wear far more formal business attire.

Even if your organizational culture allows a lot of freedom in how employees dress, overly casual attire may not be appropriate in the workplace. It's often better to play safe and dress conventionally.

Another way to help ensure you dress appropriately is to emulate the dress of successful people. Just as a junior lawyer might take cues from the top partners, you can observe and copy other professionals in your organization.

This doesn't mean simply copying the types of clothes of any successful person you know. For example, if you work in the mailroom, you shouldn't start dressing exactly like your organization's CEO.

But if you look to people at a level just above yours in the organization's hierarchy, you can determine how those who've already taken your next potential career step dress. Emulating this dress style can help send others the message you're ready to move to a higher role.

3. General guidelines

A common sense guideline for maintaining a professional image is to stay well groomed. The message sent by smart clothes can be undone by messy hair, dirty fingernails, or even body odor. These aspects of appearance are sometimes overlooked, but require attention. So don't underestimate the importance of personal grooming – and pay appropriate attention to your face, hair, hands, and odor.

See each area to learn more about it.

Face

In addition to daily face washing, men should shave daily and keep facial hair neat, including eyebrows, nose hairs, and ear canal hairs. Men should also keep a razor with them at work in case they need to shave before an evening meeting.

Mustaches and beards should be kept neatly trimmed unless religion or cultural custom dictates otherwise.

Women should wash their faces daily and ensure their makeup is understated.

Both men and women should brush their teeth at least twice daily and should consider carrying breath freshener – for example, for use after lunch or before heading into an important meeting.

Hair

For both men and women, it's vital to have clean and neat hair. Men in formal environments should generally have short, conservative hairstyles. If long hair is permitted, it should be kept in a neat ponytail. Women with long hair should keep it out of their eyes. Ponytails are neater than free hanging styles.

Hands

People notice the state of your hands, so whether you're male or female, you must ensure your hands and fingernails are clean.

Men should make sure their fingernails are short and filed. Women should wear nails shorter than a half-inch. If women use nail polish, they should ensure it's not chipped and favor conservative, neutral colors.

Odor

If you wear perfume, aftershave, or deodorant that overwhelms people you meet, you can be sure that's what they'll remember about you. So opt for subtle or neutral scents instead. Also avoid any kind of unpleasant body odor by bathing or showering every day.

Keep in mind that many work environments are scent free and prohibit the wearing of aftershaves or perfumes to protect employees who may have allergies or perfume sensitivities.

In most work environments, it's best to dress conservatively. So generally, the safest option is to stick with well-fitting, conservative clothes. Avoid loud or garish clothes that will draw people's attention away from your professional role.

It's important for men to ensure their suits fit properly and are of good quality. A suit that's scruffy, baggy, out of date, or even too flashy will be perceived as unprofessional.

Similarly, a loud tie or shirt is likely to send the wrong message. If you look at your outfit as a whole, you should be able to judge whether all the clothes work together. White socks, for example, won't ever work with a dark suit.

Women have more freedom with dress, but loud or sloppy clothing is still inappropriate. For example, a shiny, yellow suit is unlikely to convey a suitably professional image.

Unless your organization explicitly spells out a dress code, both men and women may have some freedom in choosing what to wear, and a range of outfits of different types may be suitably professional.

See each professional to learn more about appropriate outfits for men and women.

Men

It's widely accepted that men's professional dress rules are stricter than those for women. Often the expectation in a professional setting is that a man will dress formally. Men can wear any conservative-colored suit – black, navy blue, dark gray, or pinstripe – with an unobtrusive shirt and a complementary tie. The recommended shoe is the black lace-up presidential style.

As an example, a man wears a dark gray suit, a pale gray shirt, and a tie with a subtle maroon and cream spotted pattern. The shoes are black leather square-tipped lace-ups.

Women

Women may wear a pantsuit or a suit jacket with a skirt. Slacks and a jacket are usually considered better for business casual wear. Women have more color freedom than men, but anything understated is still preferred to loud colors. The recommended professional shoe is the classic pump.

A professional-looking woman wears a gray pantsuit with subtle white pinstripes, black classic pumps, and a pale pink blouse.

To avoid looking sloppy, it can help to organize your existing wardrobe. For example, start by sorting your clothes into categories – casual, professional, and to be discarded or given away.

After sorting, you can judge whether you need to purchase any new professional outfits.

In a business context, accessories and jewelry are worn more by women than by men – but regardless of gender, you should accessorize sparingly. Accessories can say a lot about your attention to detail and imagination, as well as personal taste.

For women, jewelry and hair accessories should be kept subtle and understated. The right choice can complete a particular ensemble, but something large or brash may be distracting and appear unprofessional.

It's also important to ensure your accessories and jewelry are of reasonably good quality, or they may nullify your professional image.

It's also a good idea to determine your organization's acceptable level of jewelry. For example, it may be considered inappropriate for men to wear earrings, and both men and women may be limited to wearing a single ring on each hand.

You should also consider items such as pens, briefcases, laptop bags, hats, and watches as accessories. These should be of good quality and subtle in style.

Reflect

Consider what you know about accessories and jewelry in a professional context.

How do you think body piercings and tattoos should be handled?

Enter your thoughts in the text box provided and then select the Compare button for an answer.

Write down your response or enter it in a text file in your word-processor application (or in a text editor such as Notepad) and save it to your hard drive for later viewing and for comparison with the alternate opinion that follows.

Piercings and tattoos

You may have said that although it's acceptable for women to wear one set of earrings, piercings of any other kind should be hidden or removed during work – especially when meeting with clients.

In almost all business contexts, clothing should cover all tattoos.

A further guideline for dressing professionally is to avoid showing too much skin. Many people feel that short skirts, low-riding pants, and low-cut tops don't belong in a professional environment.

Another often-overlooked guideline regarding professional dress is to keep clothes clean. It may be common sense, but for those with busy lifestyles, this does take planning. For example, a businessman working late hours for extended periods might forget to wash or launder his clothes. It's definitely not appropriate to wear stained or dirty clothing to work and it's advisable to plan ahead so that you always have a spare set of clean clothes.

If you want to look and smell professional, never wear the same clothes two days in a row. Simply put, make sure your clothes are clean and your shoes are polished.

4. BUSINESS CASUAL

A final and sometimes tricky guideline for dressing profession-ally is ensuring you don't misunderstand what's meant by "busi-ness casual." This is an ambiguous term and its meaning varies. For example, you might attend a business casual dinner in cas-ual pants and a shirt, only to find most other guests wearing suits. This would certainly make you feel uncomfortable and might even dent your professional image. If you're even slightly unsure about the appropriate attire, ask beforehand.

A danger with a business casual dress code is that it's open to abuse, whether intentional or unintentional. You should re-member that despite the "casual" part of the expression, every business casual occasion is still about business.

So don't use business casual occasions to make personal state-ments with your outfits. If you do this, you'll shift the focus away from business and your demeanor will be less profes-sional.

Because "business casual" is an ambiguous term, these individ-uals have interpreted the phrase in different ways:

- Ben, who errs on the side of caution when he's invited to what he's been told will be an informal dinner
- Charlene, who decides to attend a business casual lunch in slightly less formal, but still professional, at-tire
- James, who attends a lecture on e-banking, with a dress code specified as business casual, in weekend gear, and

- Pippa, who wears casual but neat clothes to a business casual lunch

Select each employee for more information about what message their business casual attire sends.

Ben

Ben is an accountant attending an informal dinner, which his company's CEO hosts. In line with his understanding of business casual, Ben modifies his usual work dress very slightly. He dons a white shirt, dark gray pants, polished black leather shoes, and a smart black jacket. He keeps a tie with him in case everyone else is wearing one. Ben feels he's ready for business if the situation calls for it.

Charlene

Charlene is a manager at a recruitment agency, and is invited to a business casual lunch with her managing director and several important clients. Charlene dresses down only slightly, keeping her choice of color and fabric subtle. She wears a black jacket, a white knitted top, black pants with white pinstripes, and black ankle boots, giving the message she's there for business rather than pleasure.

James

James is a programmer who works for a bank. He's invited to lecture on e-banking, with a dress code specified as business casual. He wears his weekend outfit consisting of a windbreaker, faded jeans, and sneakers. Needless to say, when he enters a room full of people with blazers and shirts, he feels underdressed. James's casual outfit may give others the impression he doesn't take them, or his work, very seriously.

Pippa

Pippa is a middle manager at an investment bank. She attends a business casual lunch with managers of other branches. Pippa focuses on the casual side of business casual and wears her favorite sweater, nail polish to match, and her most comfortable black pants. When Pippa arrives at the lunch, she sees that most people are dressed more professionally than her, leaving her embarrassed. For the entire lunch, she's afraid to give an opinion – for fear of drawing attention to her inappropriate attire.

As in the examples of James and Pippa, erring on the casual side of "business casual" can have embarrassing consequences. The most important principle to remember about business casual is to always be prepared for anything business-related.

Case Study: Question 1 of 2

Scenario

For your convenience, the case study is repeated with each question.

Cheri and Joanne work at the office of a financial advisor, liaising with clients about investment updates. Both women hope to build sound business reputations and further their careers, although they dress very differently at work.

Access the learning aid Cheri and Joanne to find out exactly how the two women dress and to help you answer the questions.

Consider what you know about professional dress and then answer the questions in any order.

Question

Considering the rules of professional dress, which statements are correct?

Options:

1. Cheri wears clothes that are too racy for her office environment
2. Joanne's clothes could use dry cleaning and her shoes need some polish
3. Joanne's outfit is a little too old and baggy to fit in with her work colleagues

4. Joanne's outfit is too casual to be considered professional

5. Cheri needs to pay more attention to her grooming because she sometimes smells a little sweaty

Answer

Option 1: *This option is correct. Cheri's outfit is too revealing and brightly colored to fit comfortably alongside the attire of her colleagues. Her jewelry is also a little more flamboyant than is usual in her office.*

Option 2: *This option is incorrect. Despite Joanne wearing a hand-me-down outfit, she keeps her clothes and shoes spotlessly clean.*

Option 3: *This is a correct option. Although it's not always noticeable, Joanne's pantsuit is clearly an old outfit that doesn't fit well. Joanne should consider wearing a slightly newer and better fitting outfit if she wants to convey a more professional image.*

Option 4: *This option is incorrect. Despite being a slightly older style, Joanne's outfit is certainly formal enough to fit in with her office.*

Option 5: *This is an incorrect option. Cheri showers daily and takes care of her grooming.*

Case Study: Question 2 of 2

Scenario

For your convenience, the case study is repeated with each question.

Cheri and Joanne work at the office of a financial advisor, liaising with clients about investment updates. Both women hope to build sound business reputations and further their careers, although they dress very differently at work.

Access the learning aid Cheri and Joanne to find out exactly how the two women dress and to help you answer the questions.

Consider what you know about professional dress and then answer the questions in any order.

Question

How can Cheri and Joanne dress more professionally?

Options:

1. Cheri should tone down her makeup
2. Joanne should trade her suit for one that fits better
3. Cheri should wear a less revealing blouse
4. Joanne needs to wear more makeup to help her stand out
5. Cheri's shoes are better suited to a cocktail party, so she should choose something less glamorous
6. Joanne should enhance her appearance with some eye-catching jewelry
7. Cheri should look to more senior colleagues in her company for pointers on how to dress

Answer

Option 1: This option is correct. Cheri's makeup is too flashy for her environment. She should choose more subtle colors and apply them more sparingly.

Option 2: This is a correct option. Joanne's outfit is old and baggy, so she should replace it with something newer and better-fitting. This will help her convey a more professional image.

Option 3: This option is correct. Cheri is currently wearing too revealing a blouse. She should replace this with something more modest and conservative.

Option 4: This option is incorrect. Joanne's subtle makeup fits well with an office environment.

Option 5: This option is correct. Cheri's shoes definitely convey glamour rather than business. She should choose a more conservative style in a darker color.

Option 6: This option is incorrect. Joanne's conservative outfit, including adornments, fits in with her office environment. She should perhaps consider getting something newer and better fitting, but not something more flashy.

Option 7: *This is a correct option. If Cheri looked to her senior colleagues, she could correctly determine an acceptable style of dress and adornment.*

In business, it's vital to ensure your appearance aligns to the professional message you want to convey. Dressing professionally will make people approach you more readily, help you command respect, and boost your self-esteem and self-confidence.

To ensure you dress professionally, you should always abide by your organization's dress code, emulate the dress style of successful people in your organization, ensure you're well-groomed, and dress conservatively. You should keep accessories to a minimum, avoid showing too much skin or wearing too much makeup, and ensure your shoes are always clean. You should also ensure you know what's meant by a "business casual" dress code and avoid dressing overly casually when this applies.

MAINTAINING A PROFESSIONAL WORKSPACE

After completing this topic, you should be able to recognize examples of appropriate workspace presentation.

1. APPROPRIATE WORKSPACE DECOR

The way you dress at work will influence other people's perceptions of how professional you are. Similarly, the way you decorate and organize your workspace will make an impression – one that can either enhance your professional image or undermine people's confidence in you. So a good question to ask yourself is "What does my workspace say about me?"

If piles of folders and papers are lying around your office, your coworkers might think you're disorganized.

Because your workspace is an extension of your image, you want it to reflect who you are in a tasteful and professional way. You want your clients to view you as competent and trustworthy. And you want your managers to view you as someone ready to advance.

Your workspace might be a cubicle in an open-plan environment, or you might have a private office behind closed doors. Either way, you should make the effort to personalize your workspace so it's pleasant to work in and creates a good impression.

When you update your workspace decor, the first thing you should do is consider your environment. Your industry, and your organization's image, will give you an indication of what type of decor is appropriate.

For example, you'd expect an investment brokerage firm to have a much more conservative image than a small graphic design company. You're not going to find creative and colorful posters, an eclectic mix of furniture, or a big-screen TV at the firm.

Instead luxury floors and chairs, neutral colors, and stylish art pieces are in order.

So in considering the image you want to convey, you need to follow the cues of your environment. What is appropriate for a bank manager is more than likely not going to work for an image consultant.

Nikki and Paul both need to personalize their workspaces. Nikki has recently been promoted and now has a private office. Paul's workspace is part of an open-plan office, and consists of a u-shaped desk with partitions that are virtually ceiling-high. One side of his workspace is open and looks out onto a public lounge area.

Select Nikki and Paul to learn more about them, and how their contexts should influence their decor choices.

Nikki

Nikki works as a consultant for a high-profile financial planning and investment company. Most of the company's clients are wealthy investors, and the company's branding and image reflect this. Silver and gray colors feature prominently in the company's logo, signage, and fittings, and most of the furniture is made from rich mahogany.

An effort has been made to ensure the characteristics of elegance, quality, and wealth are communicated. Nikki's office decor will need to be in keeping with the company's style and to reflect these same values.

Paul

Paul sells advertising space for a popular music industry magazine. The magazine has a fresh simple image that gives it the necessary versatility to cover a wide variety of genres. The company is careful to maintain a contemporary look and feel in its image and decor.

Due to the nature of his job, Paul is often out on the road and visits clients in their offices. However, the open-plan nature of his workspace means it's still important for him to maintain the same contemporary and simple theme in his decor choices as the company uses elsewhere in the office.

As well as considering your environment, you need to ensure you're familiar with any policies or regulations your company has regarding appropriate office decor. For example, your company might allow you to display images on your wall only if they're framed.

Nikki's company owns a large collection of artworks it has built up over time. It has a strict policy that employees should display only company artworks on their walls – although they may display a limited number of personal images or photographs on their desks.

For the purposes of decorating her office, Nikki has been given a catalog of all the company's art pieces. She's free to choose the ones she likes from the catalog. She decides on a series of black and white photographic images featuring various cityscapes and interesting architecture. She likes the elegant feel of the black and white prints. She also thinks that the themes of power and progress fit in well with her environment.

Paul's company has a much less rigid decor policy. Its position is that as long as decor is in keeping with the company's simple and contemporary style, employees can use their own discretion when decorating their workspaces. It does, however, stipulate that all decor is subject to the approval of management. Given his industry, Paul opts to display a series of images of musical instruments and musicians with simple black frames on the wall above his desk.

When you consider decorating your workspace, you're not restricted only to paintings and photographs. Some examples of effective decor items you might include are wall mirrors, bookcases and shelves, lighting elements, plants, desk accessories, and floor coverings.

See each decor item to learn more about it.

Mirrors

A wall mirror is a decor element you can use to great effect. With a well-chosen frame and decorative details, it can be displayed as an art piece in its own right. It also blends with virtually any room style and may make a room feel lighter and more spacious.

Bookcases and shelves

Bookcases and shelves are an effective way of adding diversity and a possible point of interest. In addition to being aesthetically attractive, the books you choose to display may assist you in your day-to-day job responsibilities.

Lighting

Supplementary light fixtures can be aesthetically pleasing and have a practical function in the office. For example, a well-chosen lamp can be an attractive desktop piece and provide focused lighting for reading or working.

Plants

Plants are an effective way to bring a natural element into your workspace. However, they do require some maintenance. You need to ensure they are watered regularly and dead or browning leaves are trimmed. Wilted and untidy plants won't help you portray a professional image. Be sure to choose plants that do well in the amount of light you have available in the office.

Desktop accessories

Various accessories may give your desktop a more organized look. For example, a well-chosen holder for your pens and pencils and an attractive table clock may help accentuate your professionalism.

Floor coverings

You probably won't be able to choose whether you want carpet, tile, or a wood finish for your basic floor covering. You can, however, complement and accentuate the basic finish with a well-chosen carpet or rug to bring in more color, or to better define an area of the office.

Nikki decides to use a section on one of her walls to display her qualification certificates. She opts for silver frames to complement the black and white photos she has selected. Paul wants to make his workspace more attractive by bringing in some plants. He decides on a leafy potted plant that will look good next to his desk, and a small bonsai tree for his desktop.

Question

Which examples demonstrate appropriate workspace presentation?

Options:

1. A realtor loves yachting and has decorated his walls extensively with boating paraphernalia such as flags, wooden oars, and buoys

2. A sales manager has a large corner bookcase with a library of titles that are well regarded in her industry

3. A fashion designer has covered most of her office's main wall with a large mirror

4. A child psychologist has just started her own practice and has been given an old fashioned ball and claw desk and chair set to use in her consulting room

5. The CEO of a furniture manufacturing company has a sound system that features prominently in his office, although it's against company policy

Answer

Option 1: This option is incorrect. While you can incorporate elements of your personal interests into your decor, in this case, the realtor has overdone it. One or two tastefully and stylishly presented

framed prints of yachts would be more appropriate.

Option 2: *This option is correct. A bookcase with relevant titles adds a sophisticated element to the office and suggests you're well read in your industry.*

Option 3: *This is a correct option. The large mirror will do a lot to make the room feel spacious and light. It's also appropriate in her industry because she can use it when fitting and showing new garments on models.*

Option 4: *This is an incorrect option. The furniture set has a very dated look and is unsuitable for a child-friendly environment, where simple styling and light and welcoming tones would be more appropriate.*

Option 5: *This is an incorrect option. Even though the CEO is the highest authority in the company, he should conform to the company's decor policy – which is intended to serve its public profile and image.*

2. MAINTAINING YOUR PROFESSIONAL IMAGE

You can take several steps to help ensure your workspace enhances your professional image. The first of these is to avoid decorating your workspace with items that undermine your professional image. Examples are toys, stuffed animals, or cute pictures of puppies or kittens, which can make you appear childish or immature. Avoid disrespectful or, what you perceive to be, humorous signs and posters. Also avoid displaying religious paraphernalia of any form. These may make your co-workers or clients uncomfortable.

A second important guideline is to avoid clutter. Clutter includes all unnecessary items taking up space on desk or table surfaces, or even on the floor. For example, it might include piles of papers and books, coffee mugs, assorted stationery items, and personal ornaments.

Reflect

What effects do you think an overly cluttered workspace can have?

Enter your thoughts in the space provided. Then select the Next Page button to learn more about why it's important to avoid clutter.

Write down your response or enter it in a text file in your word-pro-

cessor application (or in a text editor such as Notepad) and save it to your hard drive for later viewing.

As you may have noted, a cluttered workspace suggests to those who visit your office that you're disorganized and lack control over your environment and job. It's also likely to hinder your work efficiency, making it harder to find things when you need them.

When it comes to untidy workspaces, disorganized paper piles are one of the biggest culprits. You should use a filing or paper management system to keep things presentable and in order. Also consider having an empty drawer where you can quickly store your things if you have visitors.

To combat clutter, you should evaluate every item in your office, determining whether it really has to be there and whether it contributes to your professional image. You should choose new accessories in the same way. For example, don't pick up new items on the spur of the moment or use your workspace as a dumping ground for unwanted items from home.

A third guideline is to keep your workspace clean and tidy. A dirty, messy desk will reflect poorly on you and can make a work environment less pleasant for everyone.

It's best to avoid eating at your desk – but if you do, ensure you clean up any crumbs or spills, and dispose of your garbage in the kitchen rather than in your own wastebasket.

Also, if you drink coffee at your desk, use a mug rather than a disposable takeout cup, which can look sloppy.

A fourth guideline is to avoid highly-scented items in decor. The fragrances these items produce may irritate people with allergies or sinus problems – and others may simply find the scent unpleasant. And as a final guideline, avoid vulgarity, nudity, and suggestiveness in any paintings, photographs, or posters you use.

So, to maintain a workspace that enhances your professional image, you should avoid items that undermine your professional image, avoid clutter, keep your workspace clean and tidy, avoid highly-scented items, and avoid vulgarity, nudity, or suggestiveness in the decor you use.

See each guideline for examples of what is and isn't appropriate.

Avoid items that undermine your professional image

Whenever Paul finds a newspaper cartoon he particularly enjoys, he cuts it out and sticks it to the edge of his monitor. Some cartoons may be politically charged, in bad taste, or offensive in other ways – so doing this could undermine Paul's professional image.

Instead he should consider including more neutral artwork or photographs – preferably in appropriate frames – in his workspace.

Avoid clutter

Every few months, Nikki adds another framed photo of her young daughter to her desk. There's now little room left for work-related papers or files.

It's appropriate for Nikki to include some photos of her daughter in her workspace. However, she should choose just one or two recent ones in appropriate frames to prevent her workspace from becoming too cluttered.

Keep your workspace clean and tidy

Paul is highly conscientious and often works through his lunch breaks. Normally he takes just ten minutes to eat a sandwich and have some coffee at his desk. With being so busy, he has failed to notice several coffee stains on his desk and folders – and these aren't likely to make a good impression on visiting clients.

Instead Paul should consider having his lunch away from his

desk, even if this involves taking just a short break from his work.

Avoid highly-scented items

Nikki finds it refreshing to burn an incense stick in her office every now and then – especially after a weekend, when the office smells stuffy after having been shut for two days.

Although Nikki might like incense, others might find it cloying or uncomfortable. Nikki should avoid using highly-scented items to combat the stagnant smell after a weekend. Instead she should let in more fresh air – if possible – or use an odorless air freshener.

Avoid vulgarity, nudity, or suggestiveness

Nikki has a year calendar on her desk that has a tasteful line drawing of the form of a pregnant woman as its center image.

Although Nikki might feel that the image is in good taste, it depicts a nude woman and so could be offensive to some clients and coworkers. Instead Nikki should look for a calendar with a more neutral image.

WORKSPACE PRESENTATION GUIDELINES

Purpose: *Use this job aid to review the guidelines for presenting your workspace appropriately.*

When you decorate your workspace, there are several guidelines you should keep in mind:

- ask yourself what your workspace says about you
- consider the nature of the industry you're working in and match the decor you choose to this
- consider your organization's image and choose decor accordingly
- make sure you're informed of any company policies regarding appropriate office decor
- avoid items that are likely to undermine your professional image
- avoid clutter
- keep your workspace tidy and well-ordered
- avoid highly-scented items
- avoid vulgarity, nudity, or suggestiveness in images

Question

Which businesspeople have chosen to decorate their work

areas in ways likely to enhance their professional images?

Options:

1. An accountant has a desktop filing system that allows him to sort his current documents into categories based on their level of urgency

2. A marketing executive has a framed photo of her daughter hugging the family dog on her desk

3. An investment broker has supporters' paraphernalia for his favorite football team displayed all over his workspace walls

4. A publisher likes to burn an aromatic candle while she does her yoga exercises in her office during her lunch break

5. A sales representative has decorated his wall with posters from the company's previous ad campaigns, in which scantily-clad models were featured

Answer

Option 1: This option is correct. The accountant is using a filing system to avoid clutter and make sure his workspace is more organized. This will help enhance his professional image.

Option 2: This is a correct option. When used well, family photos are a great accessory for personalizing your desktop without undermining your professional image.

Option 3: This is an incorrect option. The investment broker needs to be more discreet and express his loyalty to the team he supports in ways that don't undermine his professional image.

Option 4: This option is incorrect. Although the publisher burns the candle only during her lunch break, its scent is likely to linger in the office for some time. This is inconsiderate of visiting clients and coworkers, who may have allergic reactions or simply find the scent unpleasant.

Option 5: This is an incorrect option. Although the company used

the images for advertising purposes, many clients and potential clients might consider them to be in bad taste and take offense.

3. SUMMARY

Like your own appearance and behavior, your workspace projects an image. You need to make sure its decor is appropriate, given your organization's policies and culture, your position, and the nature of the industry you're in. You want your clients, your coworkers, and your managers to view you as someone who is competent and professional. Always follow the guidelines and regulations your company might have regarding appropriate office decor.

Guidelines for ensuring your workspace enhances your professional image include avoiding items that undermine your professional image, clutter, untidiness, highly-scented items, and vulgarity, nudity, or suggestiveness in the decor you use.

PROFESSIONALISM BEYOND THE OFFICE

After completing this topic, you should be able to recognize how to conduct yourself professionally beyond the office.

1. ACTING PROFESSIONALLY OUTSIDE THE OFFICE

The world is becoming a smaller and much less private place. Everything you do can be recorded, written down, posted, and made available for the public to see, read, or hear about. Word-of-mouth spreads fast, but the Internet has made it spread even faster and to a wider audience. So now more than ever it's important to take care about what you say and do.

Donald is a junior manager at a large company. He attended a big party on the weekend and posted photographs from it on his social network profile.

Sumie, a clerk who works with Donald, sees the photographs over the weekend.

Follow along as Donald talks to Sumie about the weekend he's just had.

Donald: Hey, Sumie! How was your weekend? Wow, I had a crazy party on Saturday night. Drank way too much beer.

Donald is excited.

Sumie: Yes, I know. I was looking at some of the photos you posted. There are some rather wild pictures of you.

Sumie is slightly shocked.

Donald: Did you see the one where I'm throwing a chair into the pool?

Donald is laughing.

Sumie: I did. By the way, don't you have that board meeting today?

Sumie is serious.

Donald: Oh, the meeting! It starts in ten minutes. I better get to the boardroom. I hope nobody else has seen those photos.

Donald is grinning and laughing.

Question

Based on Donald and Sumie's conversation about Donald's party photographs from Saturday, how would you rate Donald's professionalism?

Options:

1. High
2. Medium
3. Low

Answer

Option 1: *You say Donald is highly professional. Actually, his behavior suggests the opposite. High professionalism means displaying good behavior, even outside of work. Such behavior reflects positively on your image, which can boost your credibility and enhance your career prospects.*

Option 2: *You say Donald's level of professionalism is medium. Actually, it's low. Taking part in compromising activities and making the evidence available on the Internet lowers Donald's level of professionalism. Whatever you do or say, inside or outside the office environment, can lower your image and credibility.*

Option 3: *You're correct in saying Donald is lacking in professionalism. This is because any activity can have a negative impact on your professional image. Whether the activities you take part in are inside or outside of the office doesn't matter. A lack of professionalism anywhere can diminish your credibility and even stunt your career.*

Any of the managers in Donald's company – and any of Donald's clients – could stumble upon the party photos he posted on the Internet. This could seriously undermine their confidence in Donald's professionalism. It could also influence company managers to exclude Donald when it's time to consider candidates for promotions.

The Internet and the rapid growth of social media have made it infinitely easier for people to share information with each other – and this includes private information.

So the danger isn't only in what information you make public yourself, but in what information others may reveal about you without your knowledge. Your business clients, partners, and managers may access this potentially compromising information about you.

You may think that people at work are unlikely to come across information about you on the Internet. But you'd be mistaken. Research shows that a considerable percentage of employees search online for information about their colleagues, and even about their customers. It's also becoming typical for job recruiters to research candidates over the Internet and to eliminate candidates for jobs based on any unfavorable information they find.

2. IT'S NOT JUST ABOUT YOU

An organization's image is at just as much risk as an individual's. Companies not only have to worry about negative publicity in newspapers and on the radio and television, but also on the Internet.

If an employee from a company acts unprofessionally or provides bad service to a customer, the customer can publicize that event immediately. This could have severe implications for the company.

So it's important to remember that as an employee, you represent the company you work for. And if you behave unprofessionally at any time – including outside work – this could harm both you and your company.

You should try to maintain an image of professionalism even when you're not in the office. To do this, you should remove any potentially compromising material from the Internet, refrain from making negative or disparaging comments, and maintain a sense of decorum at all times.

See each way to ensure you maintain a professional image for more information.

Remove compromising material

As far as possible, you should remove any material about you that may offend others from the Internet. This could include compromising pictures of yourself or others, any potentially offensive or compromising written material, and any negative comments you've made in response to other people's posts or pictures.

For example, if there are any nude or drunken photos of yourself on your personal social networking site, delete them. The same goes for negative comments about how your work colleagues dress.

Alternatively, you could ensure your social networking privacy settings are restricted so only close friends and family members have access to what you post.

Refrain from negative comments

It's important to refrain from making negative or disparaging comments about your employer, coworkers, superiors, or clients in any public forum.

For example, if your manager refuses to give you a day off, don't post offensive or threatening status updates about this on your social media profile. If your manager or colleagues find those comments, it could compromise your reputation and your career.

Maintain decorum

The best way to ensure no compromising information is published about you is to ensure there's nothing improper or offensive about your behavior. The way you act and treat people, even in your personal life, can impact your professional reputation. So don't say, write, or do anything that you wouldn't want printed in a newspaper or on the Internet. Apply standards of common sense and politeness, and treat everyone equally.

For example, don't use foul language in a restaurant or treat the waiter poorly. Observers may notice and think poorly of you instead. In fact, some of those observers may be fellow colleagues or customers.

Sandra and Latitia are two office administrators who work in the same office. Follow along as Latitia and Sandra have a conversation during lunch.

Sandra: Latitia, did you see Dave's comment on one of my online photos?

Sandra is surprised.

Latitia: Yes, I did actually. What he wrote was absolutely inappropriate. But I'd like you to consider deleting the photo from the site – it's quite a suggestive and provocative photo of you.

Latitia is slightly shocked.

Sandra: Oh! So, you're on his side!

Sandra is mean and sarcastic.

Latitia: No, that's not what I'm saying. I just think...

Latitia is apologetic.

Sandra: Well, I don't care. Dave's so nosey and arrogant. And you, you're just annoying.

Sandra is spiteful.

When Sandra complains about Dave's comment about one of the photos she's posted online, Latitia agrees the comment was inappropriate. However, when she lets Sandra know the photo may not be appropriate for online publication, Sandra is rude in her response, which shows she has no decorum or etiquette. Sandra even resorts to negative comments about both Dave and Latitia, which is unacceptable behavior.

Question

Which employees have taken actions to maintain their professionalism outside of the office?

Options:

1. Bill removes any inappropriate photos of himself from forums on the Internet
2. Amy avoids losing her temper in public and instead remains courteous at all times

3. Grant refrains from publicly criticizing his manager

4. Yasmin ensures she makes only justifiable, negative comments about people she knows

5. Andrew wears shirts with defamatory language printed on them when he's out of the office

Answer

Option 1: This is a correct option. Anyone might come across content posted on the Internet, so any content that's inappropriate or could damage a professional reputation should be removed.

Option 2: This option is correct. To maintain a professional image, you should always maintain a sense of decorum.

Option 3: This is a correct option. One way to protect a professional image is to avoid saying anything negative about others, especially in public.

Option 4: This option is incorrect. To maintain a professional image, you should avoid making any negative comments about others in public. People should be addressed directly and politely, even if they're behaving in ways that are inappropriate or unfair.

Option 5: This option is incorrect. You should always keep a sense of decorum, even when not in the office. The best policy is to dress based on what's generally considered appropriate in any given context.

3. SUMMARY

It's important to protect your professional image and your organization's image at all times – even outside the workplace. To do this, you should avoid making negative or disparaging comments about others, remove any compromising material you may have published from the Internet, and always maintain a sense of decorum.

RATE YOUR LEVEL OF PROFESSIONALISM

Purpose: *Use this follow-on activity to rate your level of professionalism.*

Instructions for use: To use this tool, consider which guidelines for conducting yourself professionally inside and outside of the office environment apply to you and which you may want to improve on. You can print this document or re-create the table in a word-processing or spreadsheet application and use it to complete the activity.

To be a professional, it's important that you behave professionally. People will scrutinize the way you dress, act, and talk both inside and outside of the office. So it's important to always be on your best behavior and to ensure that you don't offend anyone or diminish your credibility.

Professionalism survey	
Statement	**Yes/No**
I always abide by the organizational dress code and culture	
I dress conservatively and my clothes always fit properly	
I don't show more skin than is appropriate or wear	

too much makeup	
When given the opportunity to dress in "business casual" clothes, I still think critically about what messages my clothes send to those around me	
Decorations on my desk or in my office space don't undermine my professional image	
My office space is well organized	
My office space is clean	
I have don't have any vulgar or suggestive pictures or photographs in my office space	
I don't have any compromising photographs or content posted online	
I refrain from making negative or disparaging com- ments about others in public	
I maintain a sense of decorum at all times	
I don't inappropriately disclose or seek any private information about other people	

PROFESSIONALISM, BUSINESS ETIQUETTE, AND PERSONAL ACCOUNTABILITY

Anna works in a design agency. She was hired for the creative flair she showed in her portfolio. However, despite her talents, she's not well liked in the company because she continually submits work late, which means her colleagues have to catch up on lost time. Anna doesn't feel she needs to set herself any kind of standard of professionalism or to be held accountable to anyone else. The truth is her productivity is low and her relations with colleagues are suffering.

Have you ever worked in an organization where some people remained indifferent to their work commitments? Where they've failed to admit to their own work failures, content to let the blame fall on others? Or where they've boasted ungraciously about their successes? Professionalism, good business etiquette, and personal accountability are the attributes of high achievers. Employees who readily take responsibility for their actions and show courtesy to their colleagues inspire confidence in others and tend to be more successful.

Reliable and dedicated employees accept personal accountability for their actions and their work. This involves taking the power to succeed into their own hands, acting on their goals, and increasing their personal productivity.

In this course, you'll learn about professionalism, business etiquette, and making yourself accountable by following the four steps of the personal accountability framework:

1.	focusing your efforts by setting SMART goals, which are specific, measurable, achievable, realistic, and time-framed

2.	developing an action plan for each SMART goal by being clear on what you want to achieve, removing obstacles and limitations, and identifying subgoals

3.	managing your energies and priorities so you can focus on achieving what's important and complete everything you need to, and

4.	staying focused and re-energized, so you can avoid being distracted and tackle your goals with commitment and enthusiasm.

Professionalism, Business, and Accountability
1. Accountability and Personal Goals
2. Setting Goals and Developing an Action Plan
3. Managing Priorities and Energy
4. Staying Focused and Re-energizing

ACCOUNTABILITY AND PERSONAL GOALS

After completing this topic, you should be able to recognize an appropriate accountability goal for a given set of priorities, objectives, and passions.

1. UNDERSTANDING ACCOUNTABILITY

A team of three accountants – Andrea, Glen, and Kimberly – has prepared a financial review for presenting to the board of a company. However, the figures in the review turn out to be inaccurate because of a mistake in a formula used to calculate the cost of employee benefits. When asked how the mistake occurred and who was responsible, each accountant denies responsibility and gives reasons why the mistake wasn't his or her fault.

See each of the accountants for examples of their responses.

Andrea

"All I was responsible for was compiling end information. So I had nothing to do with calculating any formulas."

Glen

"I'm not responsible for the mistake in the formula. My main responsibility was to present the final review to the board, so I didn't have to check any formulas or figures."

Kimberly

"My role in this team was simply to provide the financial figures from all the departments. It wasn't my job to check that any formulas used were correct."

Although all three accountants were part of the team that prepared the financial review, none of them chose to accept responsibility for the outcome of the task.

In fact, all three accountants should have checked the formulas and figures in the review to ensure its accuracy before presenting it to the board.

Demonstrating good business etiquette and professionalism involves accepting full, personal accountability for your work, and for your role in furthering the overall goals of your organization.

Being accountable refers to taking complete ownership of your actions and the results they have. So even if a result of a task you're involved in is negative, you should take responsibility for your actions – regardless of whether particular mistakes were or weren't your fault.

It's not unusual for people to have good intentions but then to fail to follow through. For example, when attention is drawn to a mistake in a team meeting, it might seem easier just to keep quiet than to speak up and accept responsibility.

Taking ownership of your actions and their outcomes can be challenging, but failing to do this can have negative consequences for everyone. It can result in others not trusting you. And it can lead to sloppier work overall, low morale, and low productivity.

Reflect

Think about your own workplace. How do you think people around you may benefit from you being accountable?

Enter your thoughts in the space provided and then select the Compare button to find out about the effects of accountability on others.

Write down your response or enter it in a text file in your word-processor application (or in a text editor such as Notepad) and save it to your hard drive for later viewing and for comparison with the alternate opinion that follows.

Effects of accountability

As you may have noted, taking full responsibility for your actions and their outcomes, and following through, will have a positive effect on the people around you. You'll find that people will trust you more easily. They're more likely to use you as a role model, and take accountability for their own actions. And they're more likely to have confidence in your abilities to complete tasks and projects.

2. GOALS AND PRIORITIES

As well as taking responsibility for your actions and their outcomes, being personally accountable involves having a definite direction and being highly involved. It's these characteristics that make it possible to translate your intentions into constructive action.

You already learned about taking responsibility for your actions earlier in this topic. Now select each of the remaining two characteristics to learn more about them.

Having a definite direction

To be accountable, you have to know and believe in your organization's overall goal, which gives you a definite direction. This will influence the decisions you make and your actions. It also helps define what it is you're ultimately accountable for.

It's important that individuals at all levels of an organization understand and accept its goals. This is because if its people don't fully understand them, they won't know how to help achieve them.

Being involved

To be accountable, you have to be involved with the people around you. To do this, you need to develop and maintain adequate channels for discussion with them.

Any actions you take will affect those around you, so communicating with others about your actions is essential. The required communication may be on a small scale – such as communicating with your colleagues through regular meetings. Or it may be on a larger scale – such as the CEO of a large international company communicating with thousands of employees via e-mail and the company's intranet.

Gavin is a marketing manager for a company that produces skin-care products and that has recently decided to introduce a line of all-natural products. The company wants the advertising campaign for the new line to focus on the advantages of using natural products. It hopes to develop a reputation for being committed to natural health and well-being.

Consider how Gavin makes accountability an integral part of his job. First he ensures he's fully familiar with what his company hopes to achieve and with his role in contributing to its goal. He also schedules meetings with his marketing team to discuss the new advertising campaign. So both Gavin and his team members have a definite direction.

Gavin makes himself readily available whenever employees want to talk about ideas or discuss the campaign with him, and he organizes regular update meetings. In this way, he stays involved and open to communication.

Gavin always sticks to scheduled meetings and gives the team whatever information he promises to provide. And he takes responsibility for both his and the team's actions and results.

Question

What are the characteristics of personal accountability in an organization?

Options:

1. It requires that you take ownership of the outcomes of your actions

2. It depends on managers always making it clear exactly what employees must do

3. It's based on a clear goal or direction

4. It depends largely on managers taking responsibility for organizational results

5. It depends on constant, open communication

Answer

Option 1: This option is correct. To be accountable, you have to take full responsibility for your actions and the outcomes they have, whether these are positive or negative.

Option 2: This option is incorrect. If employees are to be accountable, they have to understand and support their organization's overall goals. However, accountability requires involvement and open communication. Highly autocratic management, with employees simply being told what to do at all times, may discourage a sense of personal accountability.

Option 3: This is a correct option. Accountability in an organization depends on all individuals knowing what actions to take and what it is they're working toward.

Option 4: This is an incorrect option. Individuals at all levels of an organization need to be accountable for goals to be met. Managers can't succeed alone and need staff at other levels to be accountable for their contributions too.

Option 5: This option is correct. For individuals to be accountable, they need to be involved and engaged. There has to be constant communication between employees, with a realization that an individual's actions affect others.

Correct answer(s):

1. It requires that you take ownership of the outcomes of your actions

3. It's based on a clear goal or direction

5. It depends on constant, open communication

One facet of accountability that's related to having a definite direction is having a clear goal for yourself. To have a clear goal, you need to know what you want, know what your priorities and passions are, and then align your goal with these priorities.

Think for a moment about the priorities in your life. These are things you're really invested in and committed to because they're priorities to you. They motivate and encourage you to perform well and to be accountable.

Once you know what your goal is, you'll be more committed to making decisions and carrying out the actions that lead to the achievement of the goal.

It's through this commitment to a goal that you're inspired to become accountable.

Note that unless you align your goal with your priorities, it's unlikely you'll commit fully to it and take responsibility for achieving it. In other words, you're less likely to commit to something if it's not of any real importance or value to you.

Consider how Heather ensures her goal and priorities align. She works as a call center agent, selling insurance policies to customers. The company wants to be the leader in its industry and call center agents are expected to sign up a minimum of ten new customers per week. Heather's personal goal, however, is to become the top call center agent in her company. She wants to achieve this by signing up at least 15 new customers per week.

To achieve her personal goal, Heather must work through lunch, but she regards forming and maintaining good relationships with colleagues as a priority. She knows that lunch is the only time she has to engage with her colleagues and to develop her relationships with them.

So to achieve her goal but still maintain good relationships with colleagues during her lunch time, Heather decides to come in to work half an hour earlier and leave half an hour later – giving her the extra time she needs to make more calls.

Heather is aware of the overall goal, or direction, of her company. This helps her develop a personal goal that's relevant and will make a positive contribution to the company's goal. And her commitment to her personal goal inspires Heather to take responsibility for her actions and their outcomes.

Question

Dale works for a large advertising agency. He's noticed that his department wastes a lot of paper, which is a waste of money. Dale considers environmental responsibility very important, so he wants to find a way to reduce the amount of paper his department throws away unnecessarily.

Which goal would be most likely to encourage Dale to become more accountable?

Options:

1. Make senior management aware of the problem and of which personnel are responsible for wasting resources

2. Monitor the situation over the next year, hoping that his organization becomes more environmentally conscious

3. Set up a paper recycling policy in his department to reduce the amount of paper wasted

4. Demand that the agency invest in electronic processes to reduce the use of paper

Answer

Option 1: This is an incorrect option. Blaming others for problems or inefficiencies isn't an example of demonstrating accountability. Instead, Dale should focus on what he can do himself to reduce the amount of wasted paper.

Option 2: This option is incorrect. Doing nothing and simply hoping that others will take responsibility for the problem isn't an example of being accountable. Instead, Dale should take action himself, ensuring this aligns with his priority of making his department more environmentally responsible.

Option 3: This is the correct option. Setting up a policy to reduce the amount of paper that's wasted is a good example of behaving with accountability. It involves taking responsibility for the problem and

taking personal action. Also, because this action aligns with Dale's priority of being environmentally responsible, he's likely to be highly committed to it and ready to accept accountability for the results.

Option 4: *This option is incorrect. It might not be feasible or cost-effective for the agency to change its current processes. Dale needs to consider his organization's overall goal and ensure his goal aligns with this. Also, being accountable involves taking personal action, rather than just making demands on others.*

Having a clear goal is a good starting point for developing personal accountability, but you then need to work on achieving that goal. To become fully accountable for your goals, you should follow the four steps of the personal accountability framework:

1.   set SMART goals – in other words, goals that are specific, measurable, attainable, realistic, and time-framed

2.   develop an action plan for achieving your goals

3.   manage your priorities and energy, and

4.   stay focused and re-energize whenever necessary

The remainder of this course will focus on the personal accountability framework and the four steps that it involves.

3. SUMMARY

Accepting accountability is part of good business etiquette and professionalism. It involves taking full responsibility for your actions and their outcomes, and committing to the overall goal of your organization. If you demonstrate accountability, people are likely to trust you more, to look to you as a role model, and to have confidence in your abilities.

To be accountable, you need to have a definite direction and to be highly engaged and involved in your work. You also need a clear, personal goal that aligns with your priorities and passions. This will motivate you to commit to your goal and to become accountable for achieving it.

SETTING GOALS AND DEVELOPING AN ACTION PLAN

After completing this topic, you should be able to recognize examples of SMART goals and to identify steps to take to develop an action plan

1. SETTING SMART GOALS

Unless you know what you want to achieve and work toward this, you're unlikely to succeed. As human beings, we crave different forms of success, personally as well as in business. However, without knowing how to set goals properly or to create an action plan, personal success will probably remain elusive and you will compromise your business colleagues by being an unreliable member of the team. Setting goals is thus the first step to success.

To be personally accountable for your actions and results at work, you have to start with a definite direction and a clear vision. In other words, you have to develop a clear long-term goal.

Reflect

What do you think makes a well-formulated goal?

Enter your thoughts in the text box provided. Then select the Next Page button to continue.

Write down your response or enter it in a text file in your word-processor application (or in a text editor such as Notepad) and save it to your hard drive for later viewing.

You may have thought a well-formulated goal is one you're able to achieve. You're right – it's more likely that you'll achieve a goal that you've thought through carefully, rather than a goal that has high aspirations but is too vague.

The most effective way of setting a goal is to structure it so it states explicitly what is to be achieved and how to measure whether you've been successful. To do this, you should use the SMART principle. SMART stands for specific, measurable, achievable, realistic, and time-framed.

See each characteristic of a SMART goal to learn more about it.

Specific

If your goal is specific, you have a clear idea of what is to be achieved and you can focus on achieving it. Conversely, vague goals are more difficult to follow through on. A goal like "I want to be the perfect employee " is so general that it's difficult to know where to start.

A more specific goal might be "Every day, I want to complete all my tasks quickly and proficiently."

Measurable

Without having a proper method by which to measure a goal, the goal is useless because you won't be able to know whether it's achieved or not. However, too much quantification is not good also. Your SMART goal should be measurable without being stifled.

For example, a goal could be, "I want to increase my web site's visibility with 100 more hits this month." A poor goal would be "I want more hits on my web site."

Achievable

An achievable goal is a goal that's within your power to attain. Achieving a goal is why you set the goal in the first place and each achieved goal makes the next goal easier. Conversely, if you set yourself a goal you'll never be able to achieve despite your best efforts, you're only setting yourself up for failure.

For example, if you're in manufacturing and you know you have the capacity to start a new product line, instead of just saying, "I want to start a new product line," an achievable goal might be "I want to capture a significant share of the market with this new product by next year."

Realistic

Apart from being achievable, your goals must also be realistic. This means you should ask yourself how likely is your goal to be met when you consider the different factors that influence its completion.

For example, it won't help saying "I want to become the number one distributor of electronics equipment" if you are currently lacking the optimum storage facilities. A realistic goal is, "I want to become a competitive distributor of electronics equipment."

Time-framed

Creating a timescale for realizing your goal is important because it gives you a sense of urgency and a constraint for completion, without which your goal may weaken over time as you lose focus and momentum.

For example, it's less useful to set a goal of becoming chairman of the board than to want to become chairman of the board within, say, three years.

Dominique is part of a team of sales executives. She hopes to improve her performance and, accordingly, decides to set herself the goal of improving her sales. She then wants to use the SMART principle to refine her goal.

Dominique begins by asking herself, "Is my goal specific?" It occurs to her that the formulation "improve my sales" is quite open-ended. She decides to make twelve big sales. This will focus her efforts on her specific performance and not a vague generalization.

Next she asks herself, "Is my goal measurable?" She decides the measurement method for her will be when each client signs off on the deals.

Now she asks herself, "Is my goal achievable?" As a sales executive with a good track record to stand by, she believes she can secure the sales.

She next asks, "Is my goal realistic?" This leads her to consider how there might not even be twelve ready clients to sell to at any given time. She changes her goal to closing four major deals.

Finally, Dominique asks herself by when she wants to attain her goal and settles on three months, giving herself a time frame.

Dominique thus decides to improve her sales by signing four major deals within three months, an achievable goal. Because the goal is now SMART, it can help Dominique be accountable for her actions and their results, motivating her and giving her a clear direction.

Question

Which examples of goals are SMART goals?

Options:

1. To finish a 60-page report in two months and aim to be promoted
2. To be the best manager
3. To sell 12 policies by the end of the month
4. To be a faultless employee
5. To increase a company's profit margin by 75%

Answer

Option 1: This option is correct. This goal lays out specifically what is to be achieved within a given time frame. The goal is specific, can be measured, is achievable, is realistic, and has a set time frame.

Option 2: This is an incorrect option. This goal is not specific enough. How can you measure what's meant by being the "best" manager? The goal isn't measurable and doesn't have a set time frame.

Option 3: This option is correct. This goal states what must be achieved and within what time frame. It is also specific because it states the number of policies. It also seems realistic.

Option 4: *This option is incorrect. This is a vague goal with no time constraint or method by which to measure it. It's therefore not possible to tell if it's achievable or not. Also, nobody is perfect, so it's not realistic.*

Option 5: *This is an incorrect option. Although this goal is specific and measurable, it lacks a time frame. It also doesn't seem realistic to expect a 75% increase in profit margins, no matter what the time frame. So it's probably also not achievable.*

2. DEVELOPING AN ACTION PLAN

Making well-formulated SMART goals is the first step in developing your professionalism and personal accountability. However, the best of goals are meaningless if you don't act on them. So the second step in developing your personal accountability is to develop an action plan for your SMART goals.

You can develop an action plan in five steps:

- develop a clear goal – in other words, develop a SMART goal
- remove obstacles you know could hamper your ability to achieve the goal
- identify and determine how to work around limiting factors
- divide your goal into smaller, more manageable components, and
- plan actions for each component so you can systematically address them as subgoals

Having a SMART goal that's clear about what you want to achieve helps put all the subsequent steps of developing an action plan into perspective. So it's the starting point for developing any action plan.

Suppose Dominique wants to be successful at her job but can't say precisely what she wants to achieve. Even if Dominique is highly motivated, it's likely she'll expend her energy unproductively in many directions.

However, once she has a SMART goal, she can begin on the remaining steps for creating an action plan designed to ensure she achieves this goal.

The second step for developing an action plan is to remove obstacles. Obstacles are events or circumstances that may prevent you from realizing your SMART goal, or that make it difficult to do so. For example, suppose your goal is to deliver finished product computer chips to a client within two days. However, your current supplier is far away and only transports by truck, not by air. You'll be challenged to remove this obstacle.

To identify your obstacles, you can ask yourself three questions:

- What's the main – or biggest – obstacle?
- What are other possible obstacles?
- How can I resolve each of the obstacles?

See each way in which to identify obstacles to find out more about it.

What's the main obstacle?

Obstacles can vary depending on your circumstances. Time delays, supplier problems, inexperience, and lack of resources are all examples of obstacles that can threaten your goal.

Consider Dominique, who wants to close four major deals within three months. Her obstacles might include competition from other sales executives or problems within her own company around delivering the goods on time.

What are other obstacles?

You should anticipate obstacles beforehand by asking yourself what kind you quickly overcome and what kind could completely destabilize your goal. You then record them in a list.

When Dominique makes a list, she realizes that one of the other obstacles is that her company doesn't have a large pool of suppliers so she may not always be able to offer her clients the best deals on the market.

How can I resolve obstacles?

Working out how to resolve obstacles is almost like creating a mini action plan in itself. Once you've defined all the obstacles, you break each down into smaller parts to identify the root cause of the obstacle.

For example, once Dominique has identified the main obstacle as unreliable, late delivery, she asks a series of questions about delivery solutions. If she discovers that lax deadlines are responsible for the late delivery, for example, Dominique must raise the matter with her company so the requisite process improvements are implemented.

The third step for developing an action plan is to identify and address limiting factors. A limiting factor is a shortcoming you have or a constraint that may make it harder to achieve your goal. Whereas you can remove an obstacle, you have to work around a limiting factor.

For example, if a manufacturer can't acquire a certain amount of raw materials, an action plan is needed.

Suppose in Dominique's case, the service that would win over Diallonics as a new client is ongoing technical support. However, Dominique's company lacks the capacity to provide long-term support services. This is a limiting factor that Dominique has to work around.

For example, it might be viable for her company to outsource, using another company to meet Diallonics' support needs.

The fourth step for developing an action plan is to divide your main goal into manageable subgoals. For example, if a middle manager's long-term goal is to become the managing director within ten years, the manager has to break this goal down into smaller parts. Bearing the long-term goal in mind, the manager might decide to set the subgoals of entering upper management within five years, improving a department's performance within one year, and implementing new processes within two months.

Dominique's SMART goal is to secure four major deals in three months. To reach this point, she first sets herself the subgoal of making sales worth $80,000 in 90 days, with discounts and high-quality merchandise.

Working backwards, she realizes to achieve the sales target within the 90 days, she needs to sign up more clients. She therefore breaks up the subgoal into its smaller components. First she needs to expand her client base within a month.

Finally, she accepts she will have to know her pitch. She sets herself a two-week goal of knowing her product thoroughly.

The final stage of developing an action plan involves acting on the subgoals you've created. You should consider what actions you can take to realize each subgoal. Consider for example the possible actions Dominique might take to realize her subgoals of making sales of $80,000, expanding her contacts within a target company, and choosing products to pitch.

See each of Dominique's subgoals to learn what actions she plans to take to achieve them.

Making sales of $80,000

To make sales of $80,000, Dominique can take different actions, including preparing objectives for the sales and contacting clients to find out when they can set up a meeting.

Expanding contacts

To expand contacts and negotiating partners, Dominique can research contacts on a database.

Choosing products to pitch

To choose which products to pitch to potential clients, Dominique must research the market thoroughly, review her company's latest engineering technologies, and determine what her clients' objectives might be.

Question

What are the steps for developing an action plan?

Options:

1. Identify and remove obstacles
2. Tell others about your goals
3. Develop a clear goal
4. Find ways around limitations
5. Compare your goal to other people's goals
6. Plan what to do to achieve each subgoal
7. Break up your goal into smaller components

Answer

Option 1: *This is a correct option. The second step for developing an action plan is to identify obstacles that could prevent you from achieving your goal and, as far as possible, to remove them.*

Option 2: *This is an incorrect option. It's unnecessary to communicate your goals to others, and doing this isn't a step in creating an action plan.*

Option 3: *This is a correct option. The first step for developing an action plan is to develop a clear, SMART goal.*

Option 4: *This is a correct option. The third step for developing an action plan is to identify limiting factors, or constraints, and determine how to work around them.*

Option 5: *This is an incorrect option. Your goal should be specific to you and your situation; you shouldn't attempt to compare it to other people's goals.*

Option 6: *This is a correct option. The fifth step for developing an action plan is to plan actions for achieving each subgoal.*

Option 7: *This is a correct option. The fourth step for developing an action plan is to divide your main goal into smaller, more manageable* *subgoals.*

3. SUMMARY

To become personally accountable for your work results, you need to start by developing a well-formulated goal. A SMART goal is one that's specific, measurable, achievable, realistic, and time-framed.

You then need to develop an action plan for achieving your SMART goal. Steps for doing this include ensuring your goal is clear, anticipating and removing obstacles, identifying and working around limiting factors, breaking your goal into smaller subgoals, and then planning what action to take to achieve each subgoal.

MANAGING PRIORITIES AND ENERGY

After completing this topic, you should be able to organize activities and tasks in a given scenario.

1. CATEGORIES OF ACTIVITIES

It's important to know what you want and how to get it. But developing a clear goal and having an action plan won't amount to anything if you don't translate what you've planned into action. It's by acting that you really take ownership – accepting accountability for achieving your goals. However, it can be challenging to ensure you complete all the activities you need to, and doing this requires that you manage your priorities and energy.

Every day consists of 24 hours – and that is the same for everyone. However, because we all have different constraints, we use those hours differently and with different amounts of energy.

Your time and energy are the main resources you can control to achieve your plans.

To use them optimally and achieve your goals, you should organize your activities in a manner that saves these resources and focuses them where they're needed most.

The activities that you need to carry out to attain a goal can be divided into three categories – maintenance activities, people activities, and creative and analytical activities.

See each category for more information.

Maintenance activities

Maintenance activities are routine tasks that have to be completed to ensure continued, normal functioning. An example is handling routine communications, such as responding to e-mail messages.

People activities

People activities are those that involve other individuals. They include activities such as negotiations, attending meetings, making presentations, networking, conducting performance appraisals, training staff, interviewing prospective staff, and dealing with complaints.

Creative and analytical activities

Creative and analytical activities include anything that involves being creative, planning, or solving problems. Examples are developing plans, producing reports and briefs, examining data and providing conclusions, assessing problems and brain-storming solutions, and developing new ideas.

Randal is a production manager at a large manufacturing company that produces computer components for industrial applications.

He has been asked to lead an internal project group to find ways to reduce production costs by 5% by the end of the next fiscal quarter.

To achieve this goal, Randal sets his own goal for the coming week. He focuses on trying to reduce costs by changing suppliers.

Randal identifies the activities he needs to complete within the week to meet his goal. He then classifies them as either a maintenance activity, people activity, or creative and analytical activity.

Select each category to learn more about how Randal categorizes his tasks.

Maintenance activity

One of the tasks Randal has on his list is monitoring inventory information. He classifies this as a maintenance activity because it is a routine task he is responsible for as production manager.

He needs to make sure daily operations don't go unattended because this could cause a drop in productivity in the long term. For example, without diligent monitoring of inventory, Randal may fail to notice that the plant doesn't have necessary materials for production, and this could cause a serious delay.

People activity

One of the tasks Randal has identified as part of the project he's been assigned is to discuss the supplier's proposals. This is an example of a people activity.

As part of the task, Randal submits the proposals for evaluation to a selection of his company's production managers and engineers. He arranges to meet with them a week later to discuss their findings. Some managers contact him with questions about the proposals before the meeting and Randal requests more information from the suppliers to resolve the queries. During the meeting, Randal is responsible for directing discussions so that this group of experts can decide on the supplier that will allow them to decrease costs while maintaining the integrity of the products they manufacture.

Creative and analytical activity

Randal has also identified the need to do a cost-benefit analysis, a creative and analytical activity that involves weighing up the costs against the expected benefits of various options. Information gathering and problem-solving are two more examples of creative and analytical activities.

For example, after undertaking the cost benefit analysis, Randal may find that it's most cost effective to order different amounts of materials from different suppliers.

Case Study: Question 1 of 1

Scenario

For your convenience, the case study is repeated with each question.

Patrick is an editor for a daily newspaper. His goal is to contribute more to the success of the newspaper by increasing the quality and the variety of copy his journalists submit and by playing a leading role in the development of new reporters.

Patrick has identified the activities he needs to complete within a week to meet his goal.

Answer the question to categorize the tasks Patrick needs to complete.

Question

Match examples of Patrick's activities to the activity types. More than one example may match to a type.

Options:

A.   Meet with a poorly performing journalist

B.   Conduct checks to ensure journalists will meet deadlines

C.   Map out the design of the next publication, and draft and write editorial piece

D.   Read articles produced by intern journalists and write feedback reports on each

Targets:

1. People activity
2. Maintenance activity
3. Creative and analytical activity

Answer

Meeting with a journalist who's performing poorly is a people activity because it involves interacting with another person.

Conducting checks to make sure articles aren't handed in too late is a maintenance activity – a routine activity for ensuring the proper functioning of the department.

Planning the design of a publication and writing an editorial piece are examples of creative and analytical activities. They require planning, organization, and creativity. Reviewing reporters' copy and writing reports on each of these is also an example of a creative and analytical activity because it involves problem-solving.

2. ORGANIZING ACTIVITIES AND TIME

When you've determined what category your activities fit into, you need to organize and schedule them to help ensure you can complete them efficiently. When scheduling activities, you should consider two factors – the time you have available to carry out each activity and how much energy each activity requires.

Considering how much time is available to complete tasks enables you to determine what activities to complete when, based on how much time you need to complete them.

Creative and analytical activities take the most time to complete because they require the highest level of concentration, so you should assign them to longer time slots in your schedule.

For instance, analyzing an environmental impact assessment and writing a report on it won't take five minutes. It's a creative and analytical task that may take a few hours to complete.

Maintenance activities require the least amount of time because they're routine, and can be performed during or between short time slots. For example, your first task of the day is to check and respond to e-mails that came in overnight.

People tasks may require short or long time slots, depending on what the task involves. Conducting training may take an entire day whereas carrying out an interview may take an hour. When allocating time for people activities, remember to add a little extra for preparation and follow-through.

Question

Patrick has to schedule various tasks for the coming week.

Which statements about the time it will take to complete each task are correct?

Options:

1. Conducting checks to ensure journalists will meet deadlines requires little time and can be spread across multiple, short time slots

2. Mapping out the design of the next publication requires plenty of time

3. Reading intern articles and writing reports on them doesn't require much time to complete

4. Drafting and writing the editorial piece will take Patrick the least amount of time

5. Meeting with a poorly performing journalist to discuss needed improvements will take a comparatively long time

Answer

Option 1: This is a correct option. Carrying out checks to make sure journalists don't miss deadlines is a routine maintenance task and so requires little time. It may also be performed across several time slots throughout the course of a day, or even on different days.

Option 2: This option is correct. Mapping out the design of a publication is a creative and analytical activity. This type of activity takes the most time to complete.

Option 3: This is an incorrect option. This task involves problem-solving and analysis, because it involves not only reading the articles, but also editing and producing feedback reports on them. This is a creative and analytical activity and therefore will take a fair amount of time to complete.

Option 4: This option is incorrect. Drafting and writing the editorial

piece is a creative and analytical activity. These activities take the most time to complete because they require the highest level of concentration.

Option 5: *This is a correct option. This people activity will take a long time to complete because it involves meeting with a journalist, providing details of a performance problem, and discussing a way forward. Patrick may also have to deal with some resistance from the journalist, which could take time to resolve.*

It's important to determine roughly how much energy is required to complete an activity so you can determine when it's best to schedule it. Generally, maintenance activities require little concentration and therefore little energy. A routine task like organizing your workspace, for instance, doesn't require much concentration or energy.

Creative and analytical tasks require the greatest amount of energy. These are tasks you'll have to concentrate on more. An example is preparing a budget forecast as part of a project plan you're proposing to the board of your company.

People tasks often require emotional energy because they involve interacting with different people.

Some tasks in this category may be quite draining and so require a lot of energy, whereas others may require less energy. For instance, meeting with an employee to discuss poor performance may involve a lot of energy. Meeting to thank an employee for a job well done would take a lot less energy.

Question

Match the required energy levels to the corresponding examples of activities. An energy level may match to more than one example.

Options:

A.   Low energy level

B.   High energy level

Targets:

1. Researching a new product idea and drafting a proposal for management
2. Sending an e-mail message to remind staff about a scheduled training session
3. Meeting with staff to discuss complaints

Answer

Researching and drafting a proposal are creative and analytical activities and therefore require concentration and a high level of energy to complete.

Sending an e-mail reminder is a routine maintenance task designed to ensure events proceed as planned. As such, it requires a low level of energy.

A meeting with an aim to resolve complaints is a people activity that requires a lot of energy and time to complete.

To schedule activities for achieving your goal as efficiently as possible, you should determine when you typically have the most and the least energy throughout the day. You can then match activities that require the most energy to the times when you have that energy, and focus on less energetic tasks at other times.

Energy levels may differ from person to person, but most people tend to have high energy levels in the morning or at the start of their work day – once they've had time to wake up properly and settle into a routine.

Energy levels drop after a couple of hours of concentrated work. This is the time to take a break and recuperate.

In the afternoon, energy levels may fluctuate and then fall to their lowest levels. This is often the time when people leave the office to go home.

For instance, Randal assesses his calendar to review the available time slots he has to complete his activities to meet his goal for the week.

When allocating activities to certain time slots, he bears in mind what his energy levels are like throughout the day. For example, he typically has the least energy between 11:00 a.m. and 12:00 p.m.

Graphic

The time slots that fall into Randal's high energy level times are Monday from 8:30 to 10:30 a.m., Wednesday from 1:30 to 2.30 p.m., and Thursday from 1:00 to 3:00 p.m. The low level time slots are Tuesday, Wednesday, and Friday from 11:00 a.m. to 12:00 p.m. His high energy level times are defined as 8:00 a.m. to 11:00 a.m. and 1:00 p.m. to 3:00 p.m. His low energy level times are defined as 11:00 a.m. to 12:00 p.m.

Randal allocates his maintenance activities to short time slots at times when he has less energy, and people activities to longer time slots, when he has more energy. He schedules creative and analytical activities to longer time slots at times when he generally has the most energy.

Question

Patrick, the newspaper editor, should consider the time it will take him to perform the activities that will help ensure he contributes to the success of the newspaper.

Match the level of energy required from Patrick to each of the activities he has to complete. An energy level may match to more than one activity.

Options:

A.   High energy level

B.   Low energy level

Targets:

1. Meeting with a poorly performing journalist to discuss needed improvements
2. Drafting and writing an editorial piece
3. Sending journalists e-mails asking for updates on whether they'll meet deadlines
4. Mapping out the design of the next publication
5. Archiving the editorials he's written during the past month

Answer

Taking part in performance-related meetings is a people activity. It will require a high level of energy, particularly emotional energy, because it involves dealing with poor performance.

Drafting and writing is a creative and analytical activity and therefore requires a lot of concentration. As such, Patrick needs to have a high level of energy when completing this task.

Requesting status updates via e-mail is a routine task that's categorized as a maintenance activity. It requires only a low level of concentration and energy.

Mapping out the design for a publication is a creative and analytical activity that requires concentration. It therefore requires a high level of energy.

Archiving work is a routine maintenance activity, which means it requires a low level of energy.

Question

During which available time slots should Patrick carry out the various activities he has to complete in the coming week?

Patrick's calendar indicates that on Monday he has a time slot available from 8:00 to 9:00 a.m. and a time slot from 2:00 to 4:00 p.m.

On Tuesday, he has a time slot available from 9:00 a.m. to 11:00 a.m. and again from 4:30 to 5:00 p.m. On Wednesday, he has a time slot available from 9:30 to 12:00 p.m. and from 4:00 to 4:30 p.m. On Thursday he has a time slot open from 2:00 to 4:00 p.m. and on Friday he has a time slot open from 1:00 to 4:00 p.m. Patrick's energy levels are highest from 9:00 a.m. to 12:00 p.m. and again from 1:00 to 4:00 p.m. His energy levels are lowest from 8:00 to 9:00 a.m. and 4:00 to 5:00 p.m. He has lunch every day between 12:00 and 1:00 p.m.

Options:

1. E-mail staff to check their progress, Monday 8:00 to 9:00 a.m.

2. Map the publication's design, Monday and Thursday, 2:00 to 4:00 p.m.

3. Read intern articles and write reports, Wednesday, 4:00 to 4:30 p.m.

4. Meet poorly performing journalist, Tuesday, 4:30 to 5:00 p.m.

5. Write editorial, Friday, 1:00 to 4:00 p.m.

Answer

Option 1: *This option is correct. Checking staff progress is a routine maintenance task and doesn't require a lot of time or energy. So a one hour slot at the start of the day from 8:00 to 9:00 a.m., when Patrick still has low energy levels, is appropriate.*

Option 2: *This is a correct option. Mapping the design of the next publication is a creative and analytical activity that requires a longer time slot and lots of energy. So two-hour slots in the afternoon on Monday and Thursday from 2:00 to 4:00 p.m. are appropriate.*

Option 3: *This option is incorrect. The time slot between 4:00 and 4:30 p.m. is too short and is at a point in the day when Patrick has little energy, which is inappropriate for a creative and analytical activity.*

Option 4: *This is an incorrect option. This people task is likely to* *require a lot of time and energy to complete. So a suitable time slot for it is Tuesday between 9:00 and 11:00 a.m.*

Option 5: *This option is correct. Writing editorials is a creative and analytical activity that requires time and energy to complete. So an appropriate time slot for it is the three hours on Friday afternoon between 1:00 and 4:00 p.m., when Patrick has high energy levels.*

3. SUMMARY

In order to achieve your goals and put your action plan into practice, you'll have to carry out certain activities. These activities are divided into three categories: maintenance, people, and creative and analytical activities.

You need to consider the time available and the required energy levels when organizing any activity. Maintenance activities require the least time to perform and the lowest level of energy. Creative and analytical activities require the most concentration, and therefore the longest time slots and the highest level of energy. Before performing people activities, you need to allocate time for preparation and follow-through. These activities require a high level of emotional energy.

Finding Your Best Times

Purpose: *Use this follow-on activity to determine the best times for completing your activities, given the energy levels they require.*

Instructions for use: To use this tool, you can print this document, or recreate it in a word processing or spreadsheet application and use it to complete this activity.

When setting out to meet your goals, it's important to organize your activities according to the required time and energy levels. To determine when the best times are for you to perform your different tasks, assess your tasks and energy levels for one week and record your findings. To do this:

- categorize each task you perform as a maintenance, people, or creative and analytical activity

- record the time of day you performed each task – for instance morning, afternoon, or evening
- record the energy level you had when you performed each task – for example high, average, or low
- determine whether you completed the task success-fully and whether you had enough energy to handle it properly at the time you chose to work on it

Activities and their related time and energy

Activity	Activity type	Time of day	Energy level	Successful?
Monday				
Tuesday				
Wednesday				
Thursday				

Friday				

STAYING FOCUSED AND RE-ENERGIZING

After completing this topic, you should be able to identify methods to stay focused and match each example to the type of energy it will help recharge.

1. STAYING FOCUSED

People often make plans and mean to stick to them, but before they know it, they've become distracted. They lose focus – and sometimes deadlines become critical and they find themselves under growing pressure. It's generally at this point that they stop accepting accountability for their actions, give up on their goals, and blame external factors for their shortcomings. Instead, you should aim to maintain your accountability and your professionalism by using particular strategies to stay focused.

Two ways to stay focused are to discourage overly sociable colleagues when you need to do your work and avoid wasting time.

Remember that even if you're distracted only for five minutes, it will take a further five or so minutes to regain your thoughts – adding up to more time wasted than you might think.

Learning how to prevent overly sociable colleagues from distracting you while trying to focus can be done in three ways. You can be honest, use the physical environment to make it clear you don't want to be interrupted, and use your body language.

See each way you can prevent overly sociable colleagues from distracting you when you need to stay focused for more information.

Be honest

Being honest with overly sociable colleagues is a direct way to try and stop them from distracting you. Respectfully point out you're busy and that you'd like to catch up with them at another time, maybe during lunch. Your honesty is likely to make them aware that you're working to a deadline. If you remain quiet, it's likely they won't even realize they're distracting you or have a negative effect on your productivity.

This isn't to say you shouldn't have any social interaction at work – but you should set aside specific times for socializing so it doesn't prevent you from achieving your work-related goals.

Use physical environment

You can use your physical environment to make it clear you'd prefer not to be interrupted. This is a slightly less direct approach than simply telling overly sociable colleagues you're busy. For example, you could do something as simple as closing your door or putting a sign on it to let everyone know you don't want to be disturbed.

If you work in an open office environment, you could try using a meeting or conference room to get away from everyone so you can focus on particular work for an hour or two.

Use body language

You can use body language to get the message across that you'd prefer not to be distracted.

For example, you can avoid making eye contact with people you know are likely to start up conversations. If you're one of those people who can listen to music and work at the same time – and it is permitted at your place of work – you could also wear earphones to discourage people from interrupting you.

Adam and Maria are both team leaders in their company. Follow along as Maria handles Adam's attempt to socialize with her when she's busy.

Adam: Morning, Maria. How are you doing?

Maria: Morning, Adam. Doing fine, thanks.

Adam: I watched such a good movie last night. You won't believe the twists and turns in it. You like thrillers, don't you?

Maria: Yes I do, and I'd love to hear about the movie, but would you mind telling me about it at lunch time? I need to finish this report before I meet with the production manager at noon today.

Maria is calm.

Adam: Oh, sorry. Sure, I'll tell you about it at lunch then.

Maria: Thanks, Adam. I'm looking forward to it!

Maria lets Adam know she needs to focus on her work instead of entering into a nonwork-related conversation. She does this without harming her relationship with Adam, because she's direct, honest, and polite. She also expresses an interest in what Adam wants to say and arranges for them to get together during lunch, when she's not busy. Adam acknowledges that Maria is busy and leaves her to get her work done.

Another important strategy is to avoid wasting too much time on routine administrative activities. Tasks such as reading and replying to e-mail messages and filing are ones you have to perform in the workplace, but they can also hamper your productivity. While you shouldn't aim to avoid these tasks, you should find ways to complete them more efficiently.

Most people receive a lot of e-mail messages, and processing them can take up a lot of time. To save time, you should organize your e-mail messages into categories, separating ones that require immediate action or replies from those that are less relevant.

Another way to minimize time spent on e-mail is to set aside specific times for checking and responding to messages, ensuring you deal with e-mail only at those times – and at most, a few times during the day.

You can also group or mark e-mails you need to reply to, and then handle all the replies at a set time during the day.

Creating an effective filing system at work can also save you a lot of time, making it faster to file documents and to find them again when you need them.

For a filing system to be effective, you should create only one file for each subject matter and store it in the correct location.

The same principles apply whether you're storing documents on paper or electronically. Files saved on your computer or laptop – like those in a physical archive – should be easy to file and to find again.

In theory, technology enables business people to send e-mail messages from their phones, have more than one project open on their computers, and have instant chats with people without leaving their desks. This is what is called technology-enabled multitasking.

However, this type of multitasking doesn't allow you to give your full attention to any one task. The relevant technologies also mean people are more vulnerable to being distracted.

Try to concentrate on one task at a time as well as one technological tool or application. Use an application because you need to, not just because you can or because it's available.

Question

What are examples of strategies you can use to stay focused on the work you need to do to achieve your goals?

Options:

1. Work in a separate conference room
2. Set up an effective filing system
3. Avoid eye contact with talkative colleagues
4. Use your cell phone to make calls at the same time as typing on your laptop
5. Deal with e-mail messages promptly, as they arrive

Answer

Option 1: *This is a correct option. By working in a separate room, such as a conference room, you'll prevent overly sociable colleagues from distracting you.*

Option 2: *This option is correct. Setting up an effective filing system will minimize the time you spend filing and searching for documents you need.*

Option 3: *This is a correct option. Avoiding eye contact with overly sociable colleagues is an example of using your body language to indicate you don't want to be distracted. This can help ensure you're left to focus on your work when you need to.*

Option 4: *This option is incorrect. Multitasking in this way involves not focusing completely on any one task. This can slow you down and distract you from getting important work done.*

Option 5: *This is an incorrect option. Rather than wasting time throughout the day checking and replying to e-mail messages, you should set aside specific times for doing this.*

2. STAYING ENERGIZED

With work pressure and various demands on your time, it's easy to become drained and exhausted. And as your energy levels start to drop, so does your productivity. Types of personal energy – all of which contribute to your ability to achieve your work goals – include physical, emotional, mental, and spiritual energy.

Select each type of energy for more information about it.

Physical

Physical energy is your body's capacity to work, or the quantity of work you're capable of completing. It depends on diet, exercise, and rest.

Emotional

Emotional energy refers to how you feel and the state of your own emotions. Good emotional energy can make you feel inspired, hopeful, and self-confident.

Mental

Mental energy determines your ability to perform mental tasks. It involves cognitive processes such as perception, reasoning, and intuition. It also influences your motivation to complete tasks, both mental and physical.

Spiritual

Spiritual energy is the energy you feel when you do something that you love doing. This is often a task you perform effortlessly. It's also derived from living according to your core values.

Each type of energy can be recharged and renewed to build up personal stamina and resilience. This will benefit both the employees and the organizations they work for. It can help avoid having to work extra hours to make up for lost time due to fatigue.

To boost your physical energy, you need to take care of your body. A good start is ensuring you get at least eight hours of sleep a night. During the day, take regular breaks – every 90 to 120 minutes – away from your desk.

You should eat small meals throughout the day, ensuring you have at least a light snack roughly every three hours.

Taking part in regular exercise at least three times a week and participating in strength training at least once a week is also beneficial, and reduces stress.

You can replenish your emotional energy by neutralizing negative emotions. One strategy for doing this is deep abdominal breathing. This can help with feelings such as impatience, anxiety, and insecurity.

You can also encourage positive emotions in yourself by expressing positive feelings, like appreciation. So next time you think someone has done a good job, go and tell this person.

When a negative situation arises, such as a conflict between you and a colleague, you should reflect on it calmly. Then take steps to diffuse the conflict. Ask yourself questions about how and why your colleague is reacting in a specific way, how important the situation is, and what you can learn from it.

To protect your mental energy, you should minimize any interruptions, especially when you're performing tasks that require a lot of concentration. Set aside times for routine activities, such as making phone calls and responding to e-mail messages, so they don't get in the way of you performing the more complex activities. At the start of each day, when you're at your most alert, identify and prioritize important challenges so they won't drain your energy levels later in the day.

The easiest way to boost your spiritual energy is to identify and do activities that you feel passionate about and that make you feel effective and fulfilled. For example, if you like working with numbers and charts, try to do more tasks that involve this.

As far as possible, dedicate time and energy to what you consider most important. After work, try to just relax and unwind before you go home. This will help clear your mind and connect better to friends or family.

Also ensure you live by your core values. For instance, if you believe in always showing up when expected, ensure you always show up on time. This will help keep your spirits high.

FOCUS AND RE-ENERGIZE

Purpose: *Use this job aid to review techniques for staying focused and energized at work.*

You can help ensure you stay focused on what's most important at work by minimizing interruptions by overly sociable colleagues and reducing the time you spend on trivial tasks.

To prevent overly sociable colleagues from distracting you:

- be honest – say you're busy
- set up a time when they can come back to talk to you
- use the physical environment to make it clear you'd prefer not to be disturbed – for example, close your office door
- use your body language – for example, avoid making eye contact with talkative colleagues

To avoid wasting time on trivial tasks:

- organize your e-mail messages
- check and respond to e-mail only at specific times during the day
- try to respond to all e-mails at one time
- set up an effective filing system
- avoid using technology to multitask – for example, avoid talking on the phone while typing an important letter

In addition, you can use particular techniques to maintain and restore four types of personal energy.

Physical energy

- get enough sleep
- take breaks away from your desk every 90 to 120 minutes
- eat regular small meals and snacks
- exercise at least three times a week

Emotional energy

- neutralize negative feelings, like impatience and anxiety, by using deep breathing
- express positive feelings, like appreciation, to others
- reflect on and diffuse conflicts

Mental energy

- minimize interruptions such as incoming e-mail and phone calls
- set specific times to respond to e-mails and phone calls
- identify important challenges and prioritize them

Spiritual energy

- identify and do tasks or activities that you are passionate about
- dedicate time to what's important to you
- live your core values

Question

Match each type of personal energy to a technique for recharging it.

Options:

A.   Physical energy

B.   Emotional energy

C.   Mental energy

D.   Spiritual energy

Targets:

1. Exercise at least three times a week
2. Diffuse conflicts effectively and reflect on them
3. Set time aside to respond to e-mails and calls
4. Dedicate time and energy to what is important to you

Answer

Exercising is an example of a technique used to recharge physical energy. Exercise reduces stress and makes you feel more awake and energetic.

Diffusing conflict is an example of a technique used to recharge emotional energy. It effectively allows you to reflect and grow from the experience.

Setting aside times for specific activities is an example of a technique used to recharge mental energy. This minimizes interruptions and allows for concentration.

Dedicating time and energy to what's important to you is an example of a technique used to recharge spiritual energy. For example, if good work relationships are important to you and you dedicate time to develop them, you're more likely to have good relationships with your colleagues.

3. SUMMARY

So you can stay focused on your goals and the work you need to do to achieve them, you should minimize distractions at work. To prevent sociable colleagues from distracting you, you can be honest, and use both the physical environment and your body language to make it clear you'd prefer not to be interrupted. To help you stay focused, you can also use strategies to reduce the time it takes to handle e-mail and filing, and avoid multitasking.

Types of personal energy include physical, emotional, mental, and spiritual energy. Each of these can be drained, resulting in a drop in productivity. However, you can use particular techniques to replenish each of the energy types.

STEPS TO PERSONAL ACCOUNTABILITY

Purpose: *Use this job aid to review the steps for improving your personal accountability.*

Personal accountability is a hallmark of professionalism. You can accept and demonstrate accountability by following four basic steps.

Step 1: Set SMART goals

Ensure your goals are formulated to achieve results by using the SMART principle. A SMART goal is one that is specific, measurable, achievable, realistic, and time-framed.

For example, if your goal is to become the perfect employee, you will struggle to know where to begin. What makes a perfect employee exactly? How will you know when you are one? Instead make a SMART goal. If you're in sales, for instance, you could say you want to make twenty major sales by the end of the year. This is specific, it can be measured, it is within your abilities, it's likely, and it has a time constraint to motivate you.

Step 2: Develop an action plan

Once you have a goal in mind, you develop an action plan to bring it to fruition in five steps:

- have a clear goal
- remove obstacles
- identify limiting factors
- divide your goal into subgoals

- plan actions for each subgoal

Step 3: Manage priorities and energy

Categorize the tasks that will help you complete your goals into three categories:

- maintenance tasks
- people tasks
- creative and analytical tasks

Then assess the time and energy required for each task.

Step 4: Stay focused and re-energized

Neutralize boisterous colleagues

Tell colleagues you don't want to be disturbed, using the physical environment and body language to do this.

Avoid time-wasting

- organize your e-mail and set aside times for handling it
- set up an effective filing system
- avoid using technology for multitasking

Understand the four types of energy

- physical
- emotional
- mental
- spiritual

COMMUNICATING WITH PROFESSIONALISM AND ETIQUETTE

The average organization consists of multiple departments and members of staff, all performing a range of different activities that need to fulfill the organization's business goals. Effective methods of communication enable these individual components to work as a unit. In other words, communication facilitates the success of the organization.

Successful communication involves both expressing and receiving information. You can think of this as input and output. Input comes in the form of messages you receive and then interpret, whereas output is what you express to others.

For a transfer of meaning to succeed, the people communicating have to share certain norms, or standards, for communication.

This is where communication etiquette comes in. It refers to the basic rules that govern communication and people's expectations surrounding it.

For example, it determines what people generally find polite and how they expect to be addressed. It also affects the ways they expect information to be presented and how they interpret this information.

In business, particular rules of etiquette have evolved for different types of communication. Generally, these rules all have a common aim – to ensure people working in business can communicate efficiently, without causing offense, misunderstandings, or unnecessary conflict.

In business, following communication etiquette will help ensure you're understood – and that you convey a professional image.

If you follow all the accepted guidelines and conventions when speaking to your colleagues, writing a business letter, or answering the phone, for example, you'll automatically inspire confidence in your professional abilities.

In this course, you'll learn more about why it's important to follow the basic rules of communication etiquette in business. You'll also learn about the rules of etiquette, as they apply to the different methods of communication:

- in person, whether with colleagues, senior members of staff, or clients
- in business writing and via e-mail
- on the telephone, and
- via online chat, voicemail, and conference calls, all of which are now widely used communication channels in business

How to Communicate Professionally
1. Communicating Professionally in Person
2. Using E-mail Appropriately in the Workplace
3. Telephone Communications in the Workplace
4. Conference Calls, Voicemail, and Online Messaging

COMMUNICATING PROFESSIONALLY IN PERSON

After completing this topic, you should be able to identify how to communicate professionally in person.

1. IMPORTANCE OF COMMUNICATION ETIQUETTE

Consider this scenario. The team lead working on an advertising campaign is expected to communicate closely with the client. However, this person's progress reports are full of errors and difficult to understand. He also comes across as overly familiar, addressing the client company's CEO by her first name and – on one occasion – using a text message to communicate important information about the cost of the campaign. The result is that the client is unimpressed and takes its future business to a different agency.

In business, unclear communication leads to aggravation and confusion, and wastes peoples' time. For example, misunderstandings and ambiguity can make it necessary to redo work completely, or to use several phone calls or e-mail messages to clarify an initial instruction.

Communicating unclearly or in ways that others consider inappropriate can also seriously damage your credibility.

So it's important to follow the basic rules of etiquette for professional communication. Your aim is to be clearly understood and project an image of professionalism in the workplace.

It's important for professional communication to be clear and succinct irrespective of what communication method you use, whether speaking to colleagues in person, by telephone, or e-mail. Also, specific rules of etiquette apply for each method of communication.

Following the proper etiquette for communicating professionally can have several benefits:

- it helps ensure messages are clear and easy to understand
- it can help nurture your professional relationships
with colleagues, subordinates, and superiors, and
- it helps develop your professional credibility

QUESTION

Why is it important to follow proper etiquette for communicating in the workplace?

Options:

1. It helps you develop credibility with friends
2. It ensures your messages won't be misunderstood
3. It enables you to cultivate professional relationships
4. It enables you to create wordy messages that make you appear more professional
5. It allows you to develop your professional credibility

Answer

Option 1: This is an incorrect option. Good communication etiquette helps you develop and nurture professional relationships with colleagues, subordinates, and superiors.

Option 2: This is a correct option. Following proper communication etiquette ensures you create clear messages that aren't misinterpreted or misunderstood.

Option 3: This option is correct. Following proper etiquette for professional communication helps you develop good professional relationships. It prevents misunderstandings, ensures communications proceed smoothly, and enhances professional credibility.

Option 4: This option is incorrect. The aim of good communication etiquette isn't to achieve professionalism through wordy messages, but to get your message across clearly and succinctly.

Option 5: This is a correct option. Adhering to proper communication etiquette helps you communicate clearly and professionally, and this will enhance your professional credibility.

2. RULES FOR COMMUNICATING IN PERSON

Communication etiquette not only varies for different methods of communication, but also between different situations. For instance, the style of communication that's appropriate for presenting departmental financial figures to company directors is different from the style used when asking a colleague for advice on how to complete a task.

So how do you know which rules of etiquette to follow in a particular situation? To determine this, you have to analyze various factors:

- company culture, which determines certain norms and expectations surrounding communication
- your audience's needs and expectations, and
- the goal of your communication – in other words, what you need to communicate and why

See each factor to learn more about how it affects the way you should communicate.

Company culture

Evaluate the company culture in which your communication takes place to determine whether it's formal or more informal, whether a structured hierarchy exists, and what the company's priorities are. These will all affect the expectations surrounding professional communication.

For instance, in a very formal organization with a strict chain of authority, it may be inappropriate to address senior managers by their first names. However, in a less formal organization, it could be considered too rigid and rather unfriendly not to use first names.

Audience's needs

You can't communicate effectively if you don't know what the people who'll receive your message need and expect.

For instance, you have to know what information your audience requires and what level of familiarity it has with a given topic. This helps determine both what you should communicate and how. Also, your audience may prefer one form of communication over another, like brief e-mails rather than detailed paper documents.

Goal of communication

You must know what you want to achieve through your communication. Your goal may be to convey information, provide training, facilitate a discussion, or argue a point. In each case, it may be appropriate to use different communication strategies.

Having a clear goal also helps ensure you can be clear, focused, and succinct.

Communicating in person is one of the most powerful ways to communicate because it lets you convey meaning using your voice, facial expressions, and body language.

However, it's important to know that specific rules of etiquette guide all face-to-face communication in professional contexts.

Follow along as Jessica, who works for an advertising agency, meets with Gilbert, a senior manager, to discuss a project she's having difficulty with.

Jessica: Brian! It's so cool of you to meet with me and help me with the project.

Gilbert: Sure Jessica, that's what I'm here for. But I'm Gilbert, not Brian. So, tell me, what problems do you want to discuss with me?

Jessica: Right, of course! I'm so bad at names. Anyway, I don't know really. Right now I just want to get this project over and done with. And Anne's supposed to help me.

Gilbert: OK. So maybe we should involve her in this meeting as well?

Jessica: Absolutely not! I don't have time for her. We just don't work well together. She really annoys me because she's picky and difficult, and is never satisfied with anything.

Gilbert: Well that's not really something we should be discussing. I thought we were meeting to discuss the difficulties you're having with the project?

Jessica: I just don't think you understand. Even the way she dresses annoys me. And I heard from someone else in the office that Anne's leaving anyway, so...

Gilbert: Jessica, I don't have time to listen to gossip about one of my staff members. You're here to do a job!

Jessica: OK, sorry. Let's chat about the project.

Question

Consider the meeting between Jessica and Gilbert. How likely, do you think, is it that Jessica will gain Gilbert's support for her project?

Options:

1. Unlikely
2. Not sure
3. Likely

Answer

Option 1: *You say it's unlikely Jessica will gain Gilbert's support.*

You're right, because the manner in which Jessica communicates with Gilbert is unprofessional. Not only does she get Gilbert's name wrong, she also tries to gossip about her colleague, and is disrespectful toward others. She uses an informal tone and slang, which makes her appear disrespectful of her senior colleague.

Option 2: *You're not sure whether Gilbert will support Jessica's project. You should reconsider your response. Because Jessica communicates in a very unprofessional manner, it's unlikely she'll gain any support from him. Not only does she get Gilbert's name wrong, she also tries to gossip about her colleague, and is disrespectful toward others. She uses an informal tone and slang, which makes her appear disrespectful of her senior colleague.*

Option 3: *You say it's likely Jessica will gain Gilbert's support despite the fact that Jessica communicates in an unprofessional manner. Consider yourself in Gilbert's situation. If your colleague gets your name wrong, tries to gossip with you, is disrespectful of others, and uses an inappropriate tone and slang, how would you feel? The likely result is that Jessica will fail to get Gilbert's support for the project.*

In her conversation with Gilbert, Jessica comes across as unprofessional and is therefore unlikely to win his support. The way you communicate in person can have a significant impact on your effectiveness and how others perceive you. Ultimately, it can affect your success in the workplace.

To communicate effectively in person, you should follow several general rules:

- use different tones when speaking to different people, according to the corporate hierarchy
- be aware of how you speak, paying attention to your tone, enunciation, pronunciation, loudness, and the correctness of the words you use
- present your message calmly, which includes controlling your body language

- show interest in what the other person is saying and focus on the topic you're discussing

- pronounce names, particularly last names, correctly, and

- be discreet and always keep office secrets to yourself

See each rule for communicating face-to-face for more information about it.

Use different tones

Although you should treat everyone with respect, the tone you use when talking to people should generally differ according to their positions in relation to you.

For example, when talking to colleagues – who are also your friends – at work, it's appropriate to use an informal tone. A more formal and polite tone is appropriate when you're addressing a superior, like a manager.

When you're speaking to a mentor or trainer, you should also use a tone that's polite and open, and ensure you ask questions and listen so that you can learn.

Be aware of how you speak

Be mindful not only of your tone, but also of how you enunciate and pronounce words, the volume at which you speak, and the accuracy of the words you use. The image you project – of yourself or your company – may be either enhanced or destroyed by the way you speak.

For example, using the wrong words or incorrect grammar, or speaking either too quietly or too loudly, can make it harder for others to understand you. It's also likely to make a poor impression.

Present your message calmly

Even in a difficult situation, it's important to communicate your message or arguments in a calm manner.

Also remember your body language sends out clear messages about what you think or how you feel. For instance, sitting or standing up straight sends the message you feel confident and at ease. Don't overuse hand gestures and try to avoid too many head movements. Facial expressions are also crucial forms of nonverbal communication. Smile when appropriate and remember to maintain eye contact with someone who's speaking to you to show you're interested and focused.

Show interest and focus

It's very distracting to talk to someone who doesn't appear interested in what you're saying. So when someone else is speaking, you should listen attentively, demonstrate you're interested, and participate in the communication. Avoid dominating the conversation, however. Instead, you should listen to what others have to say, giving them a turn to talk and responding to what they say or ask.

It's also important to remain focused on the topic of conversation, particularly in a business context. It's easy to become distracted or go off topic – and sometimes this can result in important, relevant information being diluted or missed. It's also important to avoid talking about topics that are inappropriate in the workplace, such as politics or religion.

Pronounce names correctly

It's important to ensure you know how to address people. For example, practice pronouncing the names of colleagues, superiors, clients, and clients' company names. This can save you and your company embarrassment, ensuring you don't damage your professional image by forgetting a name or pronouncing it incorrectly.

Be discreet

Being discreet requires keeping company secrets to yourself. Possible examples of company secrets are product designs, information that gives the company a competitive advantage, or information relating to staff changes such as layoffs.

You should also generally avoid disclosing any information people have confided in you, whether the information is positive or negative. For instance, colleagues may want to communicate their good news to others themselves, rather than having you pass it along. Also avoid participating in gossip.

ETIQUETTE FOR COMMUNICATING IN PERSON

Purpose: *Use this job aid to review tips for communicating professionally in person.*

There are several methods you can use to ensure you communicate effectively and professionally in person:

- adjust your tone based on the seniority of the person you're addressing
- be aware of how you speak, paying particular attention to your tone, pronunciation, enunciation, word use, and loudness
- present your message calmly, ensuring you use appropriate body language
- show interest in what others are saying and remain focused on the topic of conversation
- know and pronounce names correctly
- be discreet, keeping any office secrets to yourself

Question

What can you do to ensure you communicate professionally in person?

Options:

1. Be casual when addressing managers

2. Avoid disclosing confidential information

3. Communicate calmly, using appropriate body language

4. Use a formal tone when addressing senior staff

5. Ensure you use words correctly

6. Seek advice from coworkers about sensitive information you overhear

7. Listen attentively when others talk

8. Know how to pronounce people's names

Answer

Option 1: *This is an incorrect option. When addressing managers, you should use a suitably formal, polite tone and manner.*

Option 2: *This is a correct option. It's important to be discreet and this involves keeping company secrets and any information others confide in you to yourself.*

Option 3: *This option is correct. To communicate professionally, you need to remain calm, irrespective of the nature of your message. You also need to ensure your body language is appropriate.*

Option 4: *This option is correct. You should generally adjust your tone based on people's positions and relationships to you. For example, a more formal tone is appropriate for communicating with senior managers.*

Option 5: *This is a correct option. When communicating face-to-face, it's important to use words correctly and to be mindful of your tone, enunciation, pronunciation, and loudness.*

Option 6: *This option is incorrect. Any sensitive information or company secrets should not be passed to others. This is part of being discreet in your communication.*

Option 7: *This is a correct option. Listening attentively when someone else talks shows you're interested and focused on the conversation.*

Option 8: *This option is correct. It's important to pronounce the names of coworkers, clients, or superiors correctly to avoid embarrassment.*

3. SUMMARY

Following basic rules of etiquette for professional communication can help ensure you communicate clearly, nurture professional relationships, and develop your professional credibility.

To communicate professionally in person, you should adjust your tone according to the seniority of the person you're addressing, show interest in what others are saying, and remain calm. You should also be aware of correct word use and of how you speak, pronounce names correctly, and remain discreet at all times.

USING E-MAIL APPROPRIATELY IN THE WORKPLACE

After completing this topic, you should be able to determine whether communication etiquette for e-mail has been observed in a business setting and identify general tips for writing with professionalism and etiquette.

1. WRITING PROFESSIONAL E-MAILS

Emily works in a publishing house. She has been hoping for a promotion to the Marketing Department in one of her company's international offices. However, her application's been rejected. She may not have realized it, but the reason she didn't secure the promotion was because her application included sloppy grammatical errors and typing mistakes. These made her appear unprofessional.

If Emily had taken the time to proofread her application so it was neat, error-free, and highlighted her professionalism, it's more likely she would have secured the promotion.

Being professional in the business world means more than just meeting your deadlines or being courteous to your colleagues. It also means knowing how to communicate effectively – in writing, as well as in person.

When you consider how business correspondence is the public face of an organization, the need for proper, professional business communication becomes all the more apparent.

Effective business writing reads well, is easy to understand, and is presented in an appropriate way. General guidelines for writing professionally are to simplify your language, tailor your language to your audience, and vary your sentence construction and use lively prose. You should also proofread what you write for proper punctuation, grammar, tone, and spelling, and consider what's most appropriate in terms of document length and organization.

In business writing, it's important to use simple language so it's easy for others to understand what you want to convey. Rather than attempting to impress anyone with sophisticated vocabulary, you should aim to get to the point and say what you mean in a clear and concise manner.

You can make use of various strategies to simplify your language. These include making sure you use simple vocabulary, use concise language, avoid redundant or unnecessary words or phrases, and use the active voice.

See each strategy for simplifying your language to learn more about it.

Use simple vocabulary

Using simple vocabulary ensures better readability. For example, the sentence: "There are now mechanisms in place to facilitate the distribution of standard automobile parts," can be written much more clearly as "We're ready to begin distributing standard automobile parts."

Use concise language

Being concise helps ensure what you write is easy to understand and that you don't waste the reader's time – which is especially important in business. For example, instead of writing "A sizable number of offerings from the product range made it from the shelves in month 4," write "1,521 products were sold in April."

Avoid redundant words or phrases

You can make your writing clearer and more concise by eliminating unnecessary words or phrases. For example, rather than "the end result," just write "the result" – the end is the result.

Similarly, it's usually unnecessary to start a sentence with the phrase "there is" or "there are." Instead of writing something like

"There are three main ways to boost productivity," simply state what the ways to boost productivity are.

Use active voice

You should generally use the active voice instead of the passive voice to make your text clearer and more direct. For example, change a sentence like "The brief has been signed," to "The client has signed the brief."

When writing in a business context, you should tailor your language to your audience, taking its needs into account. For example, don't use jargon your audience is unlikely to be familiar with – but also don't explain things the audience already knows.

Also ensure you address your audience correctly and with the appropriate level of formality.

You should also be careful not to use sexist language. For example, don't refer to a person in a position of authority as "he" if you don't actually know the person's gender – and use a word like "chairperson" instead of "chairman."

You can make business writing easier to read and understand by varying the way you construct your sentences and using lively prose. You should try to mirror the natural variations common in speech. For example, alternate long sentences with short ones, and avoid starting several sentences in a sequence with the same phrase.

Consider instructions like these – "You open the file. You make the edit. You save your changes." This is stilted, and it's unnecessary to repeat the word "You" in each case.

Instead, it's better simply to write "You open the file, make the edit, and save your changes."

Proofreading your writing is essential. It enables you to identify and correct punctuation, grammar, and typing errors – all of which convey carelessness and a lack of professionalism. You should run spell checks for electronic documents, but also read what you've written. For example, it's easy to misspell a word that the spell checker doesn't pick up – and the only way you'll pick up this kind of error is by reading what you've written.

You should keep business writing as short as possible so you don't waste readers' time. So don't ramble – keep sentences to a rough maximum of about 20 one- or two-syllable words, and eliminate any redundant words or phrases. For example, "A depreciation in overall profits in the last quarter necessitated a transformation of company policy," can be rewritten simply as "Company policy has changed because of lower profits in the last quarter."

You should discuss points in the order of their importance.

Also, organize your writing so each paragraph is about a different idea.

Question

What are the general guidelines for writing professionally?

Options:

1. Keep your language simple
2. Aim to keep the reader in suspense, leaving important information for last
3. Use sophisticated vocabulary
4. Write sentences of different lengths and rhythms
5. Be sure your writing is free of any kind of errors
6. Adjust your writing based on your audience
7. Be mindful of length and organization

Answer

Option 1: *This is a correct option. Good professional writing clearly communicates what it means to say.*

Option 2: *This is an incorrect option. In business writing, you* should aim to get to the point quickly, rather than to keep the reader "in suspense."

Option 3: This option is incorrect. In business writing, you should use simple, concise language – rather than attempting to impress anyone with sophisticated vocabulary.

Option 4: This option is correct. You should vary the construction of your sentences and use lively prose to make what you write easier to read and understand.

Option 5: This is a correct option. You should proofread all your writing to ensure proper punctuation, grammar, tone, and spelling.

Option 6: This option is correct. You should tailor your writing based on the needs of your audience. For example, use an appropriate level of vocabulary and a suitable level of formality.

Option 7: This is a correct option. It's important to keep your writing as short and to the point as possible, and to organize your points logically and clearly. Generally it's best to begin with whichever points are the most important.

2. FUNCTION-RELATED E-MAIL ETIQUETTE

E-mail is a speedy and convenient form of business communication. But beware – similar to hard copy documents, you need to apply certain standards to the way you write and the way you send your e-mail messages. You would never send a prospective client a report that's riddled with spelling mistakes, is printed on an incorrect letterhead, and uses an indifferent or overly casual tone. Similarly, all e-mail communication must abide by business etiquette.

The general tips for writing professionally apply to e-mail.

In addition, specific rules of etiquette apply to business e-mail. These aren't necessarily the same rules you follow when using e-mail to communicate with family or friends.

Guidelines surrounding the use of e-mail in business relate to both its function and form.

You should remember three main function-related guidelines for writing business e-mail:

- be familiar with company policy
- don't use e-mail to avoid speaking to someone in person, and
- respond on time and leave out-of-office notes

See each guideline for more information.

Be familiar with company policy

As an employee, you need to abide by your company's e-mail policies. For instance, your company may allow the use of e-mail only for business purposes or prohibit employees from including or opening attachments above a specified file size.

Don't use e-mail to avoid speaking

It's poor etiquette to send an e-mail to someone who's sitting next to you, simply because you don't want to speak with that person face to face. E-mail shouldn't be used to depersonalize workplace relationships or drain company resources.

Leave out-of-office notes

You should always reply in good time to e-mails. Also, when you're out of the office, you should use an automatic reply feature to indicate this so that the persons e-mailing you knows roughly when to expect a response or who to contact during your absence.

Question

Calvin is a senior project manager in a financial accounting company. Access the learning aid Calvin's E-mail Use for a description of how Calvin uses e-mail and then answer the question.

What function-related rules of e-mail etiquette does Calvin follow?

Options:

1. He doesn't e-mail the person sitting next to him unless it's necessary to do so

2. He opens his e-mails when he has the time

3. He balances work e-mail with social e-mail

4. He leaves an automated out-of-office note when away

Answer

Option 1: *This is a correct option. It's good etiquette to refrain from using e-mail when the recipient is sitting next to you and it will drain company resources or sometimes be an excuse not to talk to that recipient.*

Option 2: *This is option is incorrect. It's bad etiquette to keep someone who sends you an e-mail waiting too long for a reply. In Calvin's case, he should prioritize responding to his e-mail.*

Option 3: *This is an incorrect option. Company policies often prohibit using e-mail for social purposes during work hours, as is the case at Calvin's company.*

Option 4: *This option is correct. It's a mark of professional behavior to notify others with an automated response that you'll be away. In this example, Calvin does make use of an automated reply feature to let correspondents know that he's away.*

3. FORM-RELATED E-MAIL ETIQUETTE

In an e-mail, you must follow key guidelines to ensure it meets requirements of form:

- use appropriate addressing
- always include a greeting or closing
- don't use all uppercase or lowercase
- never use offensive language
- specify the response you need
- write e-mails to show you take your job seriously
- don't use emoticons or acronyms
- use attachments for long e-mails, and
- use a professional signature

When addressing an e-mail message, it's important to ensure you use the Cc field sparingly, keep the original e-mail when responding as part of the same thread, and use the Subject field properly.

See each guideline for addressing e-mail messages for more information about it.

Use Cc sparingly

You should limit the number of respondents you carbon-copy to receive the e-mail. Too many Cc entries is disconcerting to the main recipient, creating the impression they're undervalued.

Keep e-mail thread

You should keep the whole e-mail thread when replying or forwarding e-mail. This enables participants to simply access the original or follow-up e-mails to find information they need.

Use Subject field properly

You should always insert a subject in the Subject field. A lack of a subject shows an indifference and a lack of courtesy to the person you're writing to. A subject must be succinct but specific. It can be a word, a phrase, or a sentence but should be written in sentence case with no period at the end.

When writing the main body of an e-mail, you should always include a greeting or closing with a business tone.

Don't write words in uppercase in an attempt to add emphasis. Similarly, it's inappropriate to write full sentences all in lowercase.

Also, you should never use offensive language. Don't assume something won't offend others simply because you aren't offended. Avoid misunderstandings by not including anything that could be offensive to others.

Question

You are writing an e-mail to a colleague to make a query about a tax report.

Which subject line is most appropriate?

Options:

1. Report in question
2. The tax report
3. June tax report

Answer

Option 1: This is not a correct option. This subject line is too vague.

Option 2: This option is incorrect. This can refer to any tax report and so is too vague.

Option 3: This is the correct option. The subject is succinct and specific to a tax report of a particular month.

You should specify the response you need in every e-mail so recipients are clear on what you're asking them to do. For example, Carrie's e-mailing a colleague to ask him to attend a meeting to discuss changes to the requirements of a project. She attaches the summary of the changes to her e-mail and asks him to submit any questions to her before the meeting.

When you write e-mails, show you take your job seriously by being polite and factual. Never write an angry message or use e-mail for gossip.

Business e-mails don't use emoticons, which are facial expressions made from punctuation marks commonly used in informal e-mails to show the emotions the sender is experiencing. Also, don't make excessive use of acronyms that have become standard in informal communication, such as IMO to mean "in my opinion."

You shouldn't send lengthy communications such as proposals and reports. Instead, use attachments to shorten potentially long e-mails.

As a sign of professionalism and to facilitate contacts, you should use a professional e-mail signature containing your name, your title, your company's name, your telephone number, and your company's web site address.

Question

What could you change in this e-mail to comply with the form-related rules of professional e-mail etiquette?

In an e-mail message, the address bruce@callinsure.com is entered in the To field. The Cc field contains several e-mail addresses. The Subject field is blank.

The body text reads, "Hi Bruce, Thought you'd like to know the presentation went – and the following words are written in uppercase – EXCEPTIONALLY WELL." This is followed by an emoticon of a happy face. The text continues, "Will send you more notes about it ASAP."

The closing reads, "Regards, Catherine Spiers, Senior consultant, Callinsure, Telephone 813-555-8254,www.callinsure.com."

Options:

1. Shorten the professional signature
2. Edit the recipients in the Cc field
3. Send the e-mail as an attachment
4. Remove the uppercase spelling
5. Add a subject in the Subject field
6. Remove the emoticon

Answer

Option 1: This is an incorrect option. The full professional signature is required in a professional e-mail and should contain the name and title of the sender, the company name, telephone number, and web site address.

Option 2: This option is correct. The Cc field shouldn't contain too many addresses because it might create the impression the recipient is undervalued.

Option 3: This option is incorrect. Only lengthy communications, such as reports, should be sent as attachments and this e-mail is short enough.

Option 4: This is a correct option. It's inappropriate in formal business e-mail to use social e-mail conventions such as stressing words with uppercase.

Option 5: This is a correct option. Not including a subject in the Subject field shows a lack of courtesy to the recipient of the e-mail.

Option 6: This is a correct option. In formal, business-related e-mails, you should avoid the use of the informal emoticon.

Formal letters, rather than e-mail messages, are appropriate for more serious types of communication. For example, you might use a letter to respond to a customer's complaint or to make an appointment with a potential new client. Particular rules of etiquette apply to formal business letters – which should also follow all the general rules for professional writing.

WRITING PROFESSIONAL BUSINESS LETTERS

Purpose: *Use this job aid to review when and how to write a professional business letter.*

It's common practice to use e-mail as a primary communication channel. However, when a situation is more serious – such as when you are applying for a promotion, writing to a client, or seeking funds for a new venture – you should write a formal business letter.

Guidelines for writing professional business letters can be divided into the following categories:

Letterhead

Use quality 8.5 × 11 inch paper, and ensure your company name is prominent and your contact details are clear.

Formatting

Use a font that's easy to read and a simple layout that doesn't distract from the content of the letter. Justify text to the left margin and use empty lines to separate paragraphs.

Heading

Begin with the date spelled out in full. Then include the addressee's name, title, company, street address, and finally city, state, zip code, and, if relevant, country.

Greeting

Begin with "Dear", followed by the appropriate honorific and last name – for example, Dear Mr. Brown.

Body text

Start with positive sentiments, write your main information, and end on a positive note. Don't be overly formal or use complicated language in an attempt to convey professionalism – succinct and straightforward is better.

Closing

End with "Yours truly," "Sincerely," or "Best regards," – always followed by a comma. Leave space underneath this for your signature.

Signature lines

Type the first and last name of each person who will sign the letter. Include as many signature lines as necessary.

Notation

If relevant, include two line spaces below the signature line list for Enclosures, Postscripts, and Courtesy copies.

Identifying initials

When relevant, use a line to indicate when someone other than the letter's author types and finalizes a letter. Use a colon to separate the main author's initials in uppercase from the assistant's initials in lowercase – for example, TC:sn.

Proofread

Always print out a copy of your letter and check it for errors before mailing it. Check for spelling, grammar, and a suitable tone.

Addressing

Use printed envelopes that match your letterhead and ensure you include a legible return address.

Scenario

For your convenience, the case study is repeated with each question.

Andrea works in a telecommunications company. Access the learning aid Andrea's E-mail Use for details about her use of e-mail, and then answer the questions.

Answer the questions in any order.

Question

Based on the scenario, which guidelines for professional e-mail has Andrea followed?

Options:

1. She's refrained from e-mailing someone sitting next to her

2. She's made sure she e-mails jokes to people within her organization only

3. She's left an e-mail message unopened until she felt ready to deal with it

4. She's set an automated out-of-office note for when she's away from her desk

5. She's kept her communications formal at all times

Answer

Option 1: This is a correct option. It's a waste of resources and time to e-mail someone who sits right next to you.

Option 2: This is a correct option. Andrea's company has an e-mail policy permitting social e-mails between colleagues.

Option 3: This is an incorrect option. It's bad etiquette to be tardy in opening e-mails, especially as people may be relying on you to respond to it in good time.

Option 4: This option is correct. It's a sign of professionalism to ensure people trying to send you e-mail are notified if you are away from your desk.

Option 5: This is an incorrect option. Formality is not a function requirement of office e-mailing.

Case Study: Question 2 of 2

Scenario

For your convenience, the case study is repeated with each question.

Andrea works in a telecommunications company. Access the learning aid Andrea's E-mail Use for details about her use of e-mail, and then answer the questions.

Answer the questions in any order.

Question

Based on the content of the e-mail, how has Andrea violated the basic rules of etiquette for business e-mail?

An e-mail shows the address dana@diallonics.com in the To field, and sally@earthfarm.com and tony@diallonics.com and anne@diallonics.com in the Cc field. The subject line reads "Workshop on Friday " and the body text reads "Just to finalize our travel plans for the trip to the client's HQ workshop. We leave on Friday at 11:00 a.m. and should be back by 2:00 p.m. emoticon of a smiley face.

If the travel plans change, I WILL DEFINITELY let you know ASAP." The phrase "I will definitely" is all in uppercase.

The signature reads, "Andrea Horner, Senior sales executive, Diallonics, Telephone: 608-555-7643, www.diallonics.com"

Options:

1. She has written entire words in uppercase
2. She hasn't written numbers out in full
3. She has used emoticons to convey excitement
4. She has carbon-copied too many recipients
5. She hasn't included a greeting or a closing

Answer

Option 1: *This option is correct. Andrea has written, "WILL DEFIN-ITELY" all in uppercase to emphasize it. This is overly informal and unprofessional for a business e-mail.*

Option 2: *This is an incorrect option. It's not generally necessary to write numbers out in full in business correspondence. Especially for long numbers, it can be awkward to do so.*

Option 3: *This option is correct. Emoticons aren't appropriate in business correspondence. They should be reserved for social e-mails.*

Option 4: *This option is incorrect. It's good etiquette not to include too many addresses in the Cc field of an e-mail. However, a few are acceptable and she's just used three.*

Option 5: *This is a correct option. It's important to include a courteous greeting and closing in a business e-mail. Andrea has left these out.*

4. SUMMARY

E-mail is used differently in a business context than in casual correspondence. The basic rules of any professional writing apply to e-mails, including simplifying your language and tailoring it to your audience, varying sentence construction and prose, proofreading and considering length and organization.

Guidelines specific to using e-mail in a business setting relate to both the function and form of e-mail messages. Examples of function-related guidelines are to refrain from using e-mail to avoid speaking to work colleagues directly and leaving automated out-of-office notes. Some examples of form-related guidelines are using appropriate addressing, avoiding offensive language and gossip, and including a professional signature.

Andrea's E-mail Use

Purpose: *Use this learning aid to help you answer the practice questions.*

The e-mail policy at Andrea's company encourages the use of e-mail for work-related purposes only, although some social e-mailing between work colleagues is permitted.

Andrea e-mails Dana, a colleague in another department, to mention she's made travel plans for a work-related excursion.

Instead of also e-mailing Faye, who sits next to her, she tells her in person. She then e-mails a joke to colleagues within the company.

A new e-mail message arrives from someone in another department but she decides she'll read and deal with the e-mail the next morning because she wants to catch up on filing before going home for the day.

Finally, she sets an automated out-of-office note reply for when she will be out of the office at a workshop.

1. ANSWERING THE PHONE

For many organizations, the telephone is the primary form of communication with customers. Communicating with professionalism and following the rules of good etiquette on the phone is an essential business practice, and can be just as important as communicating well in person. If you can make your clients and colleagues feel listened to and appreciated, you'll contribute to stronger business relationships.

It's important to realize that on the phone, listeners formulate their impressions of you within the first few seconds of a conversation. Just like in face-to-face meetings, first impressions count. So the way you introduce or answer a call is very important.

To make the right impression, you can apply several common best practices for answering calls:

- answer calls promptly – by the second or third ring if possible
- greet the caller and introduce yourself by stating your name
- smile when you answer your calls
- use a "telephone voice", controlling your volume and speed
- ask how you can help the caller
- use the caller's name in your conversation, and
- practice listening skills so you can be enthusiastic and

respectful in your responses

Select each practice for answering calls to learn more about it.

Answer calls promptly

Nobody likes to wait for a ringing telephone to be answered. So when possible, you should try to answer calls by the second or third ring. This will make you appear more efficient and thus more professional, and prevent callers from becoming frustrated. Answering promptly is especially important if you've prearranged a time for a call.

Greet and introduce

Your first step when answering a call should be to greet the caller and state your name. In some cases, it might be necessary to first state your company name, identify your department, and then state your name. This provides callers with a frame of reference for their interactions with you.

Smile

It's possible to hear someone smiling over the telephone – if you smile, you'll automatically sound more energetic and your tone will be warmer.

Use a "telephone voice"

You should speak clearly and slowly, although not so slowly that your speech sounds unnatural. Also keep your tone neutral and maintain an even, measured pace. This will make it easier for the person on the other side of the line to understand you.

Ask how you can help

After you've greeted the caller and introduced yourself, you should ask how you can help. You should make customers and even colleagues feel they're important to you. Asking how you can help, instead of waiting for a caller to initiate a conversation, sends the message that the caller's concerns are your priority.

Use the caller's name

Learning and using a caller's name frequently during a phone conversation shows you have taken an interest in the caller. You should politely ask for the caller's name early in the call. Record it as the person says it so you can remember it easily during the rest of the call.

Practice listening skills

The attitude you convey over the phone will help determine whether a caller reacts positively or negatively to you. You should practice good listening skills and show enthusiasm and respect during every call.

A good listening practice is to listen for unspoken thoughts the caller might have that are important to the conversation. It's also important to verify you've understood the situation accurately. You can do this using a phrase like "If I understand you correctly ..." and then summarizing what the caller has said in your own words.

Follow along as Carl handles a call from a client, Gina. Carl was careful to answer the call after two rings.

Carl: Good morning. Phlogistics Service Department. This is Carl. How can I help you?
Carl smiles.

Gina: Hi Carl, it's Gina Rosetti speaking. I'm calling to find out if the software I ordered from you has come in yet. My order number is SL25X.

Carl: Hi Gina. Thanks for the order number. Yes, I believe it's part of a shipment due in later today or first thing tomorrow. Is there anything I can help you with?

Gina: Yes...well...I...I don't really need it anymore...

Carl: Oh... Are you hoping to cancel your order?

Gina: If possible. Is it too late?

Carl: Well, the product's already on its way, so I'll need to chat to my manager first. I can't make any promises...

Gina: I understand. I just hoped it wouldn't be too late yet.

Carl: Tell me Gina, do you have a number I can call you back on this afternoon before 5 p.m.?

Gina: Sure. It's 206-555-5371.

Carl: Thanks Gina. You'll have your answer by the end of the day.

Carl handles Gina's call really well. He's quick to answer and makes sure she has a clear idea of who she's speaking to. He also picks up on the fact that Gina wants to cancel her order. By listening well, reading between the lines, and responding with enthusiasm, he's able to make a good impression. It's likely that when Gina needs a similar product in the future, she'll go to Carl's company rather than to a competitor.

Jenna recently purchased a new printer but can't get it to work. Frustrated, she calls the helpline number printed on the product's packaging. Cody is the customer service agent who receives her call. He's had a few difficult cases to deal with already and isn't in the best of moods. Follow along as he answers within three rings and greets the caller.

Cody: Sonical Group, Cody speaking. How may I help you?

Cody has a scowl on his face.

Jenna: This stupid printer doesn't want to work!

Cody: Ok...take it easy...you probably didn't read the instructions properly...

Jenna: What? Are you serious? I'll tell you about not reading instructions properly...

Cody: Sorry ma'am... Please tell me your name so that I can connect you to Fred in our IT Support Department. He'll be able to help you get this sorted out.

Question

Which statements about the way Cody handles Jenna's call are correct?

Options:

1. Although Cody's in a bad mood, he adopts a professional approach when he answers the phone promptly and greets the caller appropriately

2. Although Cody's irritated, he could do more to lighten the tone of his voice and come across with more enthusiasm

3. Cody's able to read the situation and quickly determines Jenna hasn't read the instruction manual properly

4. Cody uses Jenna's name frequently in the conversation

Answer

Option 1: This option is correct. Cody answers the call within three rings, states the company's name, introduces himself, and asks how he can help. So initially, he's following the guidelines for answering a call professionally. His tone would, however, benefit from a smile, instead of a scowl.

Option 2: This is a correct option. Cody should remember to smile. This would have come across in his initial greeting and might have helped to soften things with Jenna from the outset.

Option 3: This is an incorrect option. Cody has no way of knowing whether the customer has read the instruction manual properly or not. He jumps to conclusions and is rude in his response. He should have invited Jenna to explain her problem more clearly and then listen to her concerns.

Option 4: This option is incorrect. Cody doesn't know Jenna's name initially. He does personalize the conversation by asking for her name after he regains his composure.

2. MAKING A CALL

It's as important to make a good impression when making phone calls as it is when receiving calls.

You can follow six common best practices for making calls in a professional manner:

- prepare for the phone call before you make it
- make the call at a convenient time for your client or contact
- introduce yourself right away
- during the call, listen carefully, don't speak over the person, and answer promptly
- avoid multitasking during the conversation, and
- take notes of the conversation points

Select each best practice for making calls to learn more about it.

Prepare before

Before you pick up the phone, you should be mentally and physically prepared to make a call.

This means you should know what you want to say and have all reference materials you might need close at hand. You should know your contact's name and position, and what this person's company does. You should also ensure your environment is free of noise and distractions.

Call at a convenient time

You should time your call to avoid disturbing or overwhelming the person you're calling. For example, it may be best to avoid calling someone just five minutes after you arrive at work in the morning, or just before the end of the day – when people are often rushing to finish work. As well as being considerate, this is likely to benefit you. You're more likely to find a cooperative and engaged conversation partner if this person isn't stressed or under pressure.

When possible, you should prearrange a time to call – but let the other person know if you can't keep to this time.

Introduce yourself

When you call someone, introduce yourself in an appropriate manner and state the reason for your call. By clearly stating who you are and what you want to talk about, you equip the other person to respond appropriately.

Listen carefully and answer promptly

By listening carefully and responding promptly, you demonstrate that you value the person you're speaking to. Even if it's unintentional, interrupting others to make your own comments is rude. Instead, be patient and let the other person finish speaking before you respond.

However, it's a good idea to use simple words like "yes" and "okay" to confirm to the speaker that you're listening.

Avoid multitasking

It is important to give the other person your undivided attention. If you come across as distracted or disinterested because you're doing something else at the same time as being on the phone, you're likely to cause offense or frustration.

You should make a point of turning away from your computer and desk so that you can avoid the temptation to continue with work while you talk.

Take notes

You should take careful notes of the points made during the conversation. This will ensure the other person doesn't have to repeat information and you won't forget what was discussed.

Carl has spoken to his manager about Gina's request to cancel her order. Follow along as he returns Gina's call to respond to her request.

Gina: Hi, Gina speaking.

Carl: Hi Gina. This is Carl from Phlogistics. You called this morning about the software order you wanted to cancel. Are you able to talk now?

Gina: Now's perfect for me. I was expecting your call.

Carl: Gina, I've spoken with my manager and, although this isn't our regular practice, he's willing to cancel your order.

Gina: Oh, that's wonderful news! I was worried about it. I've just had so many other expenses in the last month – my refrigerator broke and then my washing machine stopped working and...well...thank you. This really helps me.

Carl: I'm glad it helps. Gina, I just need to get your fax number so I can send you an order cancellation form for you to sign.

Gina: Sure...let me just find it quickly... OK, my fax number is 206-555-5386.

Carl: Great, that's all I need. Is there anything else I can do for you?

Gina: No, you've been great. Thanks Carl.

Carl: Sure thing. Have a great day.

Gina: Thanks. You too.

Carl's call is professional and effective because he follows the guidelines for making calls. He phones Gina at a pre-arranged time. He's properly prepared for the call and has all the information he needs for the conversation. He also knows what information he needs from Gina. Carl's ready to take notes, including Gina's fax number. And even when Gina gets caught up in describing her financial difficulties, Carl's careful to let her finish describing her problems.

Remember Cody, who handled a call from Jenna, who was having difficulty with her printer? Company policy requires him to make follow-up calls to all customers who initially phone with queries or complaints. He's been procrastinating about calling Jenna and eventually gets to it at the end of the afternoon, just before he's due to leave the office. He opens Jenna's file so that he can make notes about the call, but returns to his card game on his computer while he dials, and almost drops the call when Jenna answers.

Follow along as Cody speaks with Jenna.

Jenna: Hi, Jenna here.

Cody: Hi Jenna. This is Cody from Sonical Group. You called a little earlier about that printer situation you were having... I just wanted to check if everything's been resolved.

Jenna: Oh, yeah... I can't really talk right now...but that Fred guy helped me out.

Cody: I'm glad to hear that. Well, I won't keep you then. Is there a better time I can call back to ask you a few questions about our service?

Jenna: Tomorrow morning.

Cody: OK. Thanks. Bye.

Question

Which statements about the way Cody handles his call to Jenna are correct?

Options:

1. Cody should realize the end of the day might not be the best time to make this call

2. Cody's prepared – he's opened Jenna's file and is ready to make additional notes in it during their conversation

3. Cody focuses his attention on Jenna's call

4. Cody doesn't introduce himself adequately at the

start of the call

Answer

Option 1: *This option is correct. Cody should have thought more carefully about a suitable time to phone Jenna. The end of the day can be quite rushed for many people as they try and finish their tasks.*

Option 2: *This is a correct option. Cody has everything he needs to take short notes during the conversation.*

Option 3: *This is an incorrect option. The computer card game distracts Cody when he starts making the call. As a result, he gets off to a poor start by nearly dropping the call.*

Option 4: *This option is incorrect. Cody introduces himself and his company, and reminds Jenna about their previous conversation. He's also clear about the reason for his call.*

3. CELL PHONE ETIQUETTE

In business, the cell phone has become an important alternative to the traditional landline telephone. It offers mobility and convenience, making it possible to communicate anywhere and at any time.

However, it also often leads callers to become unaware of themselves, others, and their surroundings. This can be unprofessional and annoying to others.

Following some basic rules of cell phone etiquette in the workplace can help ensure your behavior is professional. When making or receiving calls on a cell phone, you should use an appropriate location and choose a discreet ringtone. You should show respect by not holding personal calls during meetings or other formal gatherings. And you should avoid interrupting conversations with others to accept calls.

See each practice for good cell phone etiquette to learn more about it.

Use an appropriate location

You should try to find a location where others won't have to listen to your cell-phone conversations. A good rule of thumb is to maintain at least a ten-foot distance from anyone while you're speaking.

Choose a discreet ringtone

You should try to choose a discreet ringtone that won't be distracting for your colleagues and clients. Play it safe and choose something subtle, or use the vibration setting.

Respect formal gatherings

Never take personal calls during formal gatherings or meetings. Make sure your cell phone is switched off or set to silent mode.

Avoid interrupting conversations

Don't accept day-to-day calls when you're busy having a conversation with someone. Doing so sends the message that the unknown caller is more important than the person you are with. If you're expecting an important call, warn the person you might need to interrupt the conversation to take it.

Question

Which examples of cell phone use demonstrate good etiquette?

Options:

1. A businessperson's phone vibrates in his pocket, but he chooses to ignore it because he's listening to a presentation

2. A consultant working in an open-plan office asks the caller to hold on while she moves to a private area

3. A manager quickly switches off her cell phone after it starts ringing during a planning meeting with her supervisor

4. A sales agent uses the sound of a cheering crowd as his ringtone

5. A receptionist takes a minute to finish up a cell phone conversation so she can give her full attention to a waiting client

Answer

Option 1: This is a correct option. The businessperson shows proper respect to his colleagues in the meeting. First he's careful to ensure his phone's set to silent mode. And second, he chooses to ignore the incoming call.

Option 2: *This option is correct. The consultant's mindful of her colleagues, who would be within hearing range, and moves to a quieter area where she won't disturb anybody.*

Option 3: *This is an incorrect option. The manager should ensure her cell phone is switched off before the meeting. Although she didn't answer the call, her ringing phone is a distraction.*

Option 4: *This option is incorrect. The sound of a cheering crowd is likely to be distracting and annoying for those around the sales agent. He should choose something more subtle.*

Option 5: *This is an incorrect option. It's impolite of the receptionist to make a client wait while she finishes speaking on a cell phone. Day-to-day cell phone calls shouldn't be allowed to interfere with professional conversations.*

Case Study: Question 1 of 1

Scenario

For your convenience, the case study is repeated with each question.

Follow along as Lilian phones her supervisor, Clifford, to ask if she can have some time off the following week. She's somewhat nervous because she's calling him on the weekend.

Clifford: Hello, Clifford Rabinowitz speaking.

Lilian: Hello Mr. Rabinowitz. This is Lilian. I'm sorry to bother you on the weekend.

Clifford: Yes Lilian.

Lilian: Do you have a minute to talk with me now?

Clifford: Yes I do.

Lilian: Mr. Rabinowitz, my son is playing his first football match on Monday afternoon...do you like football?

Clifford: Yes Lilian, I do. But what can I do for you?

Lilian: Well, I'd like to take the afternoon off to go and watch.

Clifford: Monday afternoon...that's fine. It's usually pretty quiet then anyway.

Lilian: Thanks so much.

Clifford: Enjoy it.

Question

Which statements best describe Lilian's telephone etiquette?

Options:

1. Lilian's careful to introduce herself so Mr. Rabinowitz knows who he's talking to

2. Lilian should make the reason for her call clearer, instead of trying to engage him about whether he likes football

3. Lilian interrupts Mr. Rabinowitz too many times during the call

4. Lilian can't focus on the conversation because she's busy with too many other things

Answer

Option 1: This is a correct option. Lilian clearly states her name.

Option 2: This option is correct. Lilian should state the reason for her call earlier in the conversation, without digressing.

Option 3: This is an incorrect option. Lilian's polite and makes no attempt to interrupt Mr Rabinowitz.

Option 4: This option is incorrect. Lilian's completely focused on the conversation. Her problems is that she's too nervous. It would help if she had prepared for the call better.

4. SUMMARY

When you answer the telephone, you should answer promptly, introduce yourself, smile, use a "telephone voice", and ask how you can help. Also use the caller's name and listen well.

When you make a telephone call, you should be prepared, call at a convenient time, introduce yourself, answer promptly, avoid multitasking, and take notes.

Guidelines for using a cell phone include using a private location to talk, using a discreet ringtone, and ensuring you don't interrupt meetings or conversations to take calls.

CONFERENCE CALLS, VOICEMAIL, AND ONLINE MESSAGING

After completing this topic, you should be able to identify etiquette for communicating using online chat, voicemail, and conference calls.

1. VOICEMAIL ETIQUETTE

Voicemail, conference calls, and online chat all play important roles in business communication. Using the proper etiquette can increase the effectiveness of these communication channels and ensure you portray a professional image.

Voicemail includes either recording a message that callers can respond to in your absence or leaving a message for those who are unavailable to take your call. Your voicemail greeting represents you, so it needs to be professional. Guidelines for recording a professional voicemail greeting are to keep it brief, specify your details clearly, be polite and positive, and offer the caller options.

See each guideline for more information.

Keep it brief

Keep your voicemail greeting brief. Don't let your message go over 20 seconds, so you don't waste the caller's time.

Specify your details

Clearly specify your name, surname, and which department you currently work in at your company. This allows callers to know if they've contacted the correct person and department they intended to.

Be polite and positive

Be polite and positive by sitting up and being confident while recording your voicemail message. Don't record your greeting after an argument or bad news as people can hear negative tones.

Offer options

Provide the caller with options to either skip your voicemail greeting and go straight to leaving a message or to contact someone else. For instance, provide your alternate's contact options if the caller requires urgent assistance.

Respond to voicemail messages you receive as soon as possible. Alternatively, you could also state when you'll be able to respond in your voicemail greeting.

Leaving a professional voicemail message can increase the willingness and speed of a person calling you back.

Informative voicemail messages form positive impressions because the recipients will know what to expect and be at ease when it's time to call back.

Reflect

What information do you think should be included when leaving a voicemail message?

Use the text box provided to record your answer. Then select the Next Page button to learn about what you should include in voicemail messages.

Write down your response or enter it in a text file in your word-processor application (or in a text editor such as Notepad) and save it to your hard drive for later viewing.

You may have noted that when leaving a voicemail message for someone, two main components should be included. First always give your contact details, even if you've spoken to the person before as it'll save the person having to search for them.

Second, explain the reason for your call. This allows recipients to know the subject matter, access any relevant documents, and better prepare themselves for the discussion when they call back.

Don't specify the time and date of your call unless you're prompted to do this because the recipient's voicemail system usually records this automatically.

Follow along as Molly listens to Dean's voicemail greeting and then leaves a message.

Dean: Hi, you've reached Dean Wells, in the Customer Care Department at Hortalez Holdings. I'm currently unavailable, but please leave a short message, stating your query and phone number, and I'll return your call as soon as I can. Alternatively, you can contact reception at 206-555-3646.
Dean's voicemail message is playing.

Molly: Hi, Dean. I'd like to know when I can expect my package to arrive in Chicago. My reference number is UC9158812. Call me back during working hours, at 206-555-2678.

Molly is leaving a voicemail message in response so that Dean can call her back.

Dean's voicemail greeting is informative and professional. Molly's voicemail message isn't as informative because she forgets to give her name. Dean won't know who left the message or who to ask for when he calls back, unless he can track her by her reference number. If not, Dean won't be able to prepare before he returns Molly's call and he may not be able to tell her immediately when the package will arrive.

2. Conference call etiquette

Conference calls are also subject to the rules of business etiquette. This is essential because several people dial into the same phone call at once. Without any form of etiquette, this type of communication could become awkward and confusing. To ensure this doesn't happen, you should announce your name, use the mute feature appropriately, and minimize background noise.

See each guideline for more information.

Announce your name

Always announce your name clearly when you join a conference call. The other callers need to know who's listening to them. You should also identify yourself each time you speak during a conference call to prevent any confusion.

Use the mute feature

During a conference call, you should put your phone on mute if you're not speaking. You'll still hear the conversation but other participants won't be distracted by any background noise from your location. When it's time for you to speak, turn off the mute feature.

Minimize background noise

Background noise from each person's location can be distracting and make it difficult to hear what's being said. So before participating in a conference call, you should try to find a quiet venue and do what you can to minimize any background noise.

3. ONLINE CHAT ETIQUETTE

Although online chat is an easy and informal way for employees to communicate with each other, certain rules of etiquette do apply. Like a face-to-face conversation, an online chat should start and end with a polite greeting and farewell. Online chat responses should be brief and designed to encourage two-way communication. If one party has a lot to say, a better choice would be to e-mail, phone, or to meet face-to-face.

An example online chat proceeds as follows:

"Hello. How are you?"
"Good thanks."
"When can I expect the end-of-month report?"
"In the next hour or so."
"That's great! I'll come over then."
"Okay, good bye."
"Bye."

Be considerate of people who you're trying to have online chats with. Remember they're at work and may be too busy to reply immediately, so be patient.

The "nudge" function shakes the other person's online chat window and makes a sound to get attention for a response. This should be used sparingly and only if an urgent response is needed.

Question

When using conference calls, online chat, and voicemail what etiquette is appropriate?

Options:

1. Always leave your contact details when leaving a voicemail message for others
2. In a voicemail greeting, provide an alternative contact in case a caller needs urgent assistance
3. Be considerate and patient when waiting for online chat responses
4. Always provide your telephone number in the voicemail greeting you record on your phone
5. Announce your name each time you speak during a conference call
6. Give long and informative responses in online chats

Answer

Option 1: This option is correct. You should leave your full name and contact details in any voicemail message you leave to make it easy for the person you've called to phone you back.

Option 2: This is a correct option. The voicemail message you record should provide callers with the contact details for someone else who may be able to assist them when you're unavailable.

Option 3: This option is correct. People are generally at work when you're trying to contact them via online chat, so they may be too busy to reply to you right away.

Option 4: This is an incorrect option. If callers manage to reach your phone and hear the voicemail message you've recorded, it means they already have your phone number.

Option 5: This option is correct. You should identify yourself each time you speak during a conference call so the listeners know who is speaking.

Option 6: This is an incorrect option. Online chats are meant to be quick. If you have a lot to say to a colleague, it's best to do this in person, on the phone, or by e-mail.

4. SUMMARY

It's important to follow basic rules of etiquette for using voice-mail, conference calls, and online chat. You should ensure a voicemail greeting you record is short and polite, states your details, and offers options to the caller. In a voicemail message you leave for someone else, you should specify the reason for your call and your contact details.

During conference calls, you should identify yourself, minimize background noise, and use the mute function whenever necessary.

Online chats should be short conversations that start and end with pleasantries. In an online chat, don't over-use "nudging" and wait patiently for responses.

USING BUSINESS ETIQUETTE TO BUILD PROFESSIONAL RELATIONSHIPS

Good relationships with your coworkers are vital for a productive work environment. But these types of relationships don't just happen – you need to build them and constantly work at maintaining them. Developing strong professional relationships can benefit both you and your coworkers, and improve your ability to meet your business and career goals.

It's essential to observe basic business etiquette if you're to build and manage work relationships successfully.

Business etiquette refers to an unspoken set of rules and expectations for behavior in a work context.

In this course, you'll learn how to create a positive first impression on others in the workplace by observing particular rules of etiquette. This sets the foundation for building strong, lasting professional relationships.

After making an initial impression, you can support and develop your work relationships using the appropriate etiquette. In this course, you'll learn how to develop work relationships by applying three basic rules of etiquette – be polite and cooperative, keep conversation professional, and show respect.

Another important aspect of maintaining good work relationships is knowing how to defuse conflicts professionally. This course will teach you how to do this, helping ensure that the way you handle conflicts with work associates doesn't damage your relationships, but ultimately strengthens them.

Once you've completed this course, you'll be better equipped to interact with people at work in ways that strengthen your professional credibility and enhance your success.

Building Professional Relationships
1. Etiquette for a Positive First Impression
2. Developing Relationships Using Etiquette
3. Defusing Conflicts Professionally
4. Practice: Building Office Relationships

ETIQUETTE FOR A POSITIVE FIRST IMPRESSION

After completing this topic, you should be able to recognize how to make a good first impression.

1. THE IMPORTANCE OF ETIQUETTE

The way you interact with others at work will determine how they feel about you, and whether they find it easy to work with and support you in your role. If you don't follow basic etiquette, you'll find it difficult to build healthy work relationships – and it's likely you'll suffer professionally as a result. Take Carrie for example. She's a new project manager who's been asked to collaborate on a large project with Ed. Ed's one of the company's most experienced project managers.

Follow along as Carrie interrupts Ed while he's speaking to a business associate on his cell phone.

Ed: Yes, the delivery needs to be made today. I spoke...

Ed is speaking on his cell phone.

Carrie: Hi, Ed...can I talk to you?

Ed: Oh, um...I'm sorry Pete, I'll have to phone you back. Yes, thanks Pete.

Carrie: Oops – sorry to interrupt. Was that an important call?

Ed: Eh...yes actually. Can I help you?

Carrie: Well yes. I had some questions about the preliminary budget that needed to be resolved immediately, but you were nowhere to be found. I don't think it's fair for you to come in late without letting your colleagues know.

Carrie made a very poor impression on Ed. It was rude of her to interrupt his business call. It was also inappropriate for her to ask Ed if it was an important call, even though she apologizes. This isn't any of Carrie's business.

Finally, Carrie shouldn't have questioned Ed about being late for work. Ed may have had a good reason, and it's not her responsibility to tell her colleagues they need to inform her if they will be late.

As a result of Carrie's general rudeness and lack of friendliness, Ed may be unlikely to want to work with her in the coming weeks.

Reflect

Consider what Ed must think of Carrie, based on the way she interacted with him.

Why do you think etiquette is important for building work relationships?

Enter your thoughts in the text box provided, and then select the Next Page button to continue.

Write down your response or enter it in a text file in your word-processor application (or in a text editor such as Notepad) and save it to your hard drive for later viewing.

You may have noted that what you do at work – including the way you treat other people and present yourself – creates an impression. If you follow good business etiquette, you'll gain a reputation as someone who's professional, friendly, and pleasant to work with. You'll enhance your credibility and earn support from others.

Professional relationships can be difficult to navigate, especially with boundaries becoming more relaxed and lines of communication becoming less clear in many business cultures. Knowing and following the proper business etiquette can help you manage these relationships, ensuring your behavior is appropriate.

Observing good business etiquette involves two main principles:

- respecting your colleagues, and
- making sure people feel comfortable around you

See each aspect of business etiquette for more information about it.

Respecting your colleagues

It's necessary to understand and respect others if you're to build relationships with them. Observing proper business etiquette demonstrates your respect for those you interact with. It can help you develop professional relationships and benefit from the opportunities they bring.

Making people feel comfortable

Following proper business etiquette ensures you don't offend others or make them feel awkward by behaving in unexpected or inappropriate ways. It helps ensure you feel comfortable around others and others feel comfortable around you.

When individuals fail in their positions at work, it's most often because of problems in the way they interact with others. For example, when employees are fired, it's often for reasons like poor attitude, inappropriate behavior, or difficulties with interpersonal relationships – rather than lack of technical ability.

Someone who has excellent technical skills but often argues with colleagues and causes emotional upset is more likely to be fired than someone who works well with others, but has only adequate technical skills.

Following the proper business etiquette can help reduce misunderstandings and the types of mistakes that could damage your career.

2. MAKING A GOOD FIRST IMPRESSION

You can build strong work relationships by applying good business etiquette at all times. When you meet someone for the first time, you need to make a good first impression. Once you've managed to create a good first impression, you need to follow proper etiquette to develop and support that relationship. This will also help you manage challenging situations and defuse conflicts that may arise.

The first impression you make can have a lasting impact on your business relationships. To help you achieve that good first impression, you can follow eight simple rules of business etiquette. For example, one rule is that you should always be punctual. It's rude to keep someone waiting. Work out how long it takes you to get to your destination, and allow a little extra time. It's better to arrive slightly early than to arrive late.

When you meet someone for the first time, this person will form an impression of you in the first three seconds. This is why it's important to smile. By smiling, you indicate that you're positive and friendly.

It's also important to offer a handshake and to make eye contact. This is generally expected in business contexts, and helps convey your openness and confidence.

Question

Ashley is due to meet Mark, who'll be supervising the project team she's joining, for the first time. She arrives at Mark's office a few minutes early. Ashley is quite nervous, which she hides by putting on a serious expression. She greets Mark by introducing herself and offering a handshake while making eye contact.

What else could Ashley have done?

Options:

1. Ask Mark to take a seat
2. Bring Mark a token of appreciation
3. Smile while introducing herself
4. Explain that she's nervous

Answer

Option 1: This is an incorrect option. It wouldn't be appropriate for Ashley to ask Mark to take a seat in his own office. It would be up to Mark to offer Ashley a seat.

Option 2: This option is incorrect. Bringing a token of appreciation doesn't necessarily create a good impression. It can be perceived negatively as a type of bribery. When you first meet someone, you must make sure you're on time, offer to shake hands, and smile.

Option 3: This is the correct option. When meeting someone for the first time, you should remember to smile. Ashley didn't do this, perhaps because she's nervous. A smile could put both her and Mark at ease and show she's friendly and willing to communicate openly.

Option 4: This is an incorrect option. It's common for people to be nervous about first meetings, but Ashley will make a more professional impression if she comes across as confident and in control. She can make sure she's on time, offer to shake hands, and smile to make a good impression on Mark. This may help her relax as well.

When you meet someone, it's important to be open, confident, and positive. A person can tell a lot from your body language so make sure you give a firm handshake, make eye contact, keep your arms uncrossed, and smile. These behaviors will also help the other person to feel at ease. Make sure you're aware of any nervous habits you may have – such as clearing your throat or fidgeting – and take steps to control or minimize them.

You should also be polite and engaging. For example, show you're listening to what the other person is saying. You can show you're attentive by making an effort to learn something about the other person beforehand and then bring it up in your conversation. Another way is by asking questions about what you've discovered about the person.

It's important to relax and be yourself when you're introduced to someone. The more you relax, the more the other person will relax too. This will help ensure your meeting flows smoothly.

Observing the proper etiquette for business introductions doesn't mean you have to put aside your own personality. Instead, you can be yourself.

Because it's natural for people to form opinions based on first appearances, it's especially important to dress and groom yourself appropriately so that you appear neat and tidy. Clean, pressed clothes and groomed hair can go a long way in helping you portray a professional image.

A final guideline for handling business introductions is to use small talk to help put everyone at ease. Engaging in small talk establishes a connection, before you and the other person broach more serious or work-related topics. You can initiate small talk with questions. Effective small talk means conversation partners take turns talking and don't alienate each other in any way.

See each small-talk guideline for more information about it.

Initiate with questions

You can initiate small talk by asking questions about neutral topics, such as the weather or an item of news you think might interest the other person – provided the news isn't about something potentially controversial or sensitive.

Take turns talking

Small talk is effective for building rapport only if each person has a chance to talk and you don't interrupt each other. The dialog should move back and forth fairly swiftly, with each person responding to what the other has said.

Don't alienate each other

You shouldn't alienate people with professional or social backgrounds that differ from your own. For example, don't talk about something the other person might not know about or have any experience in. Instead, stick to topics that are likely to be of common interest.

Consider this example. Graham is due to meet Norman for an interview. He makes sure he dresses smartly, styles his hair neatly, and shaves before the meeting.

Follow along as Graham meets Norman for the first time.

Graham: Hello, I'm Graham. I'm here for the interview.

Graham smiles and makes direct eye contact with Norman.

Norman: Hi Graham, I'm Norman. You're right on time!

Norman and Graham shake hands.

Graham: Yes – I've been looking forward to meeting you

Norman: Well, it's great to have you here.

Graham: Thanks. Can you believe the rain? I hope you didn't get caught in it.

Norman: It came down so hard early this morning some of our streets were flooded. I'm glad I decided not to ride my bike to work today.

Graham: Oh really...do you usually ride your bike?

Graham follows all the etiquette rules associated with creating a good first impression. He greets Norman with a handshake and a smile, and makes eye contact. He's polite and his body language is welcoming. He's clearly relaxed and confident. Also,

Graham initiates small talk by commenting on the weather, and then engages with Norman by asking a question in response to what Norman says.

Although first impressions are important, you shouldn't rely on them alone. This is because first impressions of people can be misleading.

It's important to build rapport and develop relationships over time, always following the proper etiquette to support this process.

Question

Fiona and Luke are delegates from different departments and are about to meet for the first time at a conference. Still at home, Fiona realizes she's running late, so she doesn't have time to iron her blouse. She briefly practices talking in the mirror because she knows she sometimes has a nervous habit of avoiding eye contact. Fiona arrives for the conference only a couple of minutes late.

Access the learning aid Fiona and Luke to help you answer this question.

Is Fiona likely to make an overall good impression, and why?

Options:

1. Yes, because she smiles, offers a handshake, and is confident

2. No, because she's not punctual and doesn't dress appropriately

3. Yes, because she engages with Luke, controls her nervous habit, and uses small talk

4. No, because she fails to offer Luke a chair and isn't sufficiently polite

Answer

Fiona did a number of things right, but a few breaches of business etiquette keep her from making a good impression overall.

Option 1: *This is an incorrect option. It's good that Fiona smiles, offers a handshake, and appears confident. However, she's slightly late for the meeting and isn't dressed appropriately, so it's unlikely she'll make a good first impression.*

Option 2: *This is the correct option. Fiona is late for the meeting and isn't appropriately dressed. As a result, it's unlikely she'll make a good first impression.*

Option 3: *This is an incorrect option. It's good that Fiona controls her nervous habit and uses small talk with Luke. However, she isn't punctual or dressed appropriately for the conference, so it's unlikely she'll make a good first impression.*

Option 4: *This option is incorrect. It's not necessary for Fiona to offer Luke a chair. However, it would be polite for Fiona to thank Luke for offering her a seat. Also, she's late for the conference and isn't dressed appropriately. She does remember to smile, offer a handshake, and engage in small talk.*

3. SUMMARY

To build effective relationships at work, you need to follow proper business etiquette for interacting with others. This can help you manage professional relationships appropriately, demonstrate respect for others, and make them feel comfortable. It can also prevent misunderstandings and enhance your professional credibility.

First impressions can have a lasting effect on work relationships. To make a good first impression, you should be punctual, smile, offer a handshake, be open, confident, and positive, and be polite. You should also be relaxed, dress appropriately, and use small talk to build rapport.

DEVELOPING RELATIONSHIPS USING ETIQUETTE

After completing this topic, you should be able to recognize the workplace etiquette that supports relationships.

1. Politeness and cooperation

Relationships are key to business success. Once you've made a positive first impression, you can use business etiquette to help build healthy work relationships. At this stage, it's essential to develop rapport, and to behave with trust and integrity.

There are three stages of building strong relationships: making a good first impression, following proper etiquette, and managing challenging situations.

Practicing and nurturing your social intelligence can help you do this. Social intelligence refers to how you manage your interactions with other people, how well you get along with them, and how effective you are at getting them to cooperate with you.

People with high social intelligence interact in a way that draws others to them. They make others feel empowered, appreciated, and respected.

Conversely, people with low social intelligence interact in ways that tend to drive others away, or make them feel intimidated, frustrated, and devalued.

Reflect

How socially intelligent do you think you are? What could you do to improve your social intelligence in the workplace?

Enter your thoughts in the space provided, and then select Next Page to find out how you can develop your social intelligence.

Write down your response or enter it in a text file in your word-processor application (or in a text editor such as Notepad) and save it to your hard drive for later viewing.

You may have noted that to enhance your social intelligence, you can follow certain rules of business etiquette, such as being polite and cooperative, keeping conversation professional, and showing respect.

Politeness involves basic common sense and common courtesy – you should say "please" when making requests and thank people when they've met a request or done something for you.

To be polite, you should also avoid informal terms, such as "buddy," when addressing people. Always call people by their names.

Every person you interact with has feelings, from the lowest levels of the organization up to top executives and owners. It's important to be polite to people at all levels.

Often in business, you need to handle introductions. For example, you might introduce a new employee to a team member, or you may be introduced to a new client. Business etiquette includes specific guidelines for handling introductions politely:

- introduce the more senior or older person first – what this means is that the higher-ranking person should be introduced first; if two persons are at the same rank, the older person should be introduced first.
- use first and last names in your introduction

- when you're introduced to people, use small talk to put everyone at ease – for example, ask how they are, and
- don't hesitate to ask people to remind you of their names if you forget them

Peggy, the human resources manager at an accounting firm, is helping Curtis, a new employee, settle into the company. Follow along as she introduces him to Ralph, the company's president.

Peggy: This is Ralph McCall, our president. Ralph's been with us for over 30 years now.

Curtis: Nice to meet you, Mr. McCall. I'm Curtis...McGregor. How are you?

Curtis is nervous and shaking Ralph's hand.

Ralph: I'm great, Curtis! And call me Ralph. No need to be formal.

Curtis: Thanks, Ralph.

Curtis is polite and smiling.

Ralph: How are you enjoying your orientation so far? I'm sure Peggy's doing an excellent job.

Curtis: Oh yes. She's given me a great overview of the company.

Question

Which guidelines for polite business introductions were illustrated in the dialogue you just heard?

Options:

1. Ask names if you forget
2. Introduce the more senior or older person first
3. Use small talk to put everyone at ease
4. Use first and last names in your introduction

Answer

Option 1: *This is an incorrect option. Although it's good practice to ask for a reminder of someone's name if you forget, in the preceding dialogue, no one forgot names.*

Option 2: *This option is correct. Peggy introduces Ralph, the older and higher-ranking person, first in the conversation. Even if Ralph had been younger than Curtis, Peggy would have introduced Ralph first because he is more senior in rank within the company.*

Option 3: *This option is correct. After the introductions were made, Ralph and Curtis engaged in small talk which is a great way to begin to develop the relationship.*

Option 4: *This is a correct option. Peggy used Ralph's full name when introducing him to Curtis, and Curtis then introduced himself to Ralph using his first and last name.*

In the work environment, people often need to collaborate or help each other. In this regard, try to always be considerate of your colleagues – both when they need your help and when you need their help.

See each situation for more information about how you can show consideration.

When they need help

You may be busy when colleagues come to you for help or information. In such cases, stop work on your current task and give your colleagues your full attention. Don't continue working while you're talking to them, and don't give the impression they're not welcome at your desk.

It's also important to apply this principle when colleagues call you on the phone. If you continue typing on your keyboard or sound distracted, it will alert the person calling to the fact that you'd rather be doing something else, and this is impolite.

When you need help

To complete some of your tasks, you might need assistance from your colleagues. When this is the case, it's best not to impose on them, and not to expect their help instantly. Remember your colleagues also have their own work to do, and they may be stressed or pressed for time.

When you need information or help from others, keep this in mind and make sure you approach them in a polite, considerate manner that doesn't convey an air of entitlement or expectancy. And, unless a matter is extremely urgent, allow them to assist you at a time that's convenient for them.

Another way of showing consideration is to celebrate colleagues' special occasions, such as birthdays. Even if you're busy, the least you can do is make a short appearance to convey your good wishes.

It's also very important to avoid "turfism" – or behaving as if you're the master of a professional domain, and feeling threatened when others want to share that domain.

Geoff, a senior sales executive at a telecommunications company, has just stormed into the office of Hugh, another sales executive at the company. Follow along as Geoff confronts Hugh for an example of "turfism."

Geoff: I saw your little e-mail. What exactly are you trying to do?
Geoff is spiteful and angry.

Hugh: Geoff...Hi. What e-mail do you mean?

Hugh is shocked.

Geoff: The one about the V739 marketing strategy! Where you expect me to give you ideas for your campaign!

Geoff is angry.

Hugh: Oh...OK. Well, I've been struggling to sell the new model, so I wanted to know why yours was doing so well. That's all.

Hugh is explaining to pacify Geoff.

Geoff: Look, Hugh, I work very hard at making sales campaigns that work. That's why I'm the leading salesperson here. No way am I going to give my secrets away to you!

Geoff is proud and defiant.

Hugh: I'm not trying to take your spot, Geoff! I just need a little help. We need to improve the sales on these models, but I can't come up with the right strategy.

Hugh is frustrated.

Geoff: Well, your team will have to do its own work.

Geoff is stubborn.

In this example, Geoff views the top sales rank as his "turf," so he doesn't want to help Hugh in any way that could threaten that position. His selfish behavior is rude and detrimental to the company – Hugh's success would boost overall company sales. To avoid turfism like this, you should be cooperative and share your knowledge and expertise with those who come to you for advice or help.

2. PROFESSIONAL CONVERSATION AND RESPECT

You can enhance your working relationships by always being conscious of the way you converse with others. One aspect of keeping conversations professional is to avoid saying things that could offend others.

For example, don't tell offensive jokes, and don't make statements or use language that furthers offensive stereotypes about particular groups of people.

Everyone's threshold for "offensive" is different – some people may be offended by things that others are not offended by. So it's better to always err on the side of caution.

Also try to avoid sensitive subjects that could elicit strong reactions. Conversations about things like politics or other people's private lives might antagonize others or lead to misunderstandings.

Although it may be difficult, try not to let your personal problems affect your interactions with people at work. Showing excessive sadness might negatively affect others around you. And if you're in a bad mood, your choice of words, tone of voice, and body language might make your colleagues uncomfortable.

For example, if you're furious about another driver hitting your vehicle on the way to work, you might come to work angry and, as a result, behave inappropriately.

In this case, you may be tempted to vent your frustration on an innocent colleague who has nothing to do with your personal situation.

Question

Which snippets or statements are examples of unprofessional conversation in a work environment?

Options:

1. "I have enough problems at home. I don't need you giving me more to worry about right now."
2. "A lawyer and a banker walk into an office..."
3. "Like they say, examine what is said, not who speaks."
4. "Socialism is the only solution to the problems we're facing today."
5. "I don't agree with the policy, but I'm willing to discuss it with you."

Answer

Option 1: This is a correct option. This reaction is inappropriate because it brings personal problems to the office, and dismisses a colleague based on that frustration.

Option 2: This option is correct. This is an introduction to a joke that is likely to draw on stereotypes that people may find offensive.

Option 3: This is an incorrect option. This proverbial statement isn't offensive and doesn't touch on a sensitive subject, so it's not unprofessional.

Option 4: This option is correct. This statement is inappropriate in the workplace because it expresses a political view, which may antagonize or offend those who hold opposing political views.

Option 5: This option is incorrect. This statement is strong but still open-minded, so it's not inappropriate or unprofessional.

Good business etiquette also includes showing respect to everyone you interact with – whether in view of others or in private. One aspect of this is to keep your physical interactions appropriate for the office environment. For example, kissing – even on the cheek – is generally unacceptable in business settings. Instead, use a more appropriate gesture like a handshake.

It's also important to be sensitive to coworkers' needs for privacy and to respect their personal space – even if you and they work in an open-plan office.

Guidelines associated with respecting the personal space of others relate to your colleagues' work, noise levels, and personal conversations.

See each issue to learn about its guidelines.

Colleagues' work

Always consider that your colleagues may be busy when you need to speak to them, and that it's rude to interrupt them without announcing yourself first. So before walking in to speak to a colleague, always knock to signal that you're there. This applies whether your colleague has a private office or a cubicle.

Noise level

Be conscious of the level of noise you generate during your working day. Noise comes from a variety of sources, such as speaking to others, both in person and on the phone, using furniture – like opening and closing drawers – and listening to music, even if you're using earphones. Always try to keep your noise levels down so that you don't disturb those who work close to you.

Personal conversations

If you work in a cubicle, don't hold personal conversations there. If you need to speak to a colleague about a private matter, go to a quiet place away from other employees. And if you need to have a personal conversation on the phone, take the call in a private room or use your cell phone outside the office.

If you're in a colleague's office or cubicle when this person needs to take a personal call, excuse yourself to give the person privacy.

If it's handled incorrectly, criticism can cause unnecessary harm to work relationships. Take the case of Geoff, the sales executive who previously felt threatened by Hugh's request for help. The two have been paired to work on promoting a new product for their company, and Geoff isn't happy about some of the work that Hugh is doing.

Geoff meets Hugh in the crowded cafeteria at lunchtime and decides to address the issue. Follow along as Geoff confronts Hugh.

Geoff: Hugh, there's something I'd like to talk to you about.

Geoff is concerned.

Hugh: Sure. What's up?

Hugh is surprised.

Geoff: Well... your last marketing presentation was full of mistakes, including some really basic spelling and typing errors. I'm worried that your incompetence is going to make a bad impression on clients.

Geoff is frustrated.

Hugh: You're out of line, Geoff. For your information, I heard the client is impressed with my report.

Hugh is upset.

Geoff: Are you serious?! Well...anyway, all I'm saying is, you really need to check your work. Run spell checks at least!

Geoff is antagonistic.

Hugh: I don't why you're attacking me, but what you're saying isn't fair. I think it might be better if we didn't work together.

Hugh is very upset.

In this case, Geoff criticizes Hugh using unnecessarily harsh words like "incompetence" and a disrespectful tone. He doesn't specify exactly what the mistakes were. And to make things worse, he does this in front of other employees. He fails to show respect for Hugh, who naturally reacts in a defensive way. The result is that their working relationship is likely to be even more strained in the future.

As a rule, never criticize someone at work unless that criticism is justified and likely to help that person. And even then, you should deliver criticism sensitively, in private, and together with relevant praise, instead of focusing only on the negative.

See each guideline for delivering criticism for more information about it.

Sensitively

When you need to criticize others, always be sensitive to their feelings. Don't use harsh or derogatory words, and don't make them feel incompetent, stupid, or worthless. You should do your best to use words, a tone of voice, and body language that's encouraging and positive. This will help ensure you get your message across effectively, without causing hurt or making the other person defensive.

In private

Nobody likes to be criticized, and it's even worse when that criticism happens in front of other people. Public criticism can make a person feel disgraced.

Private criticism is much more likely to result in positive change. So if you have to criticize someone, try to speak to this person in a private area – away from others.

Together with praise

If you need to criticize someone, you should start off by praising good aspects of this person's work or behavior. Then respectfully put forward your criticism, specifying exactly what the problems are. Last you should try to end on a positive note, encouraging the other person or giving further praise.

This approach helps ensure that criticism doesn't leave others feeling demoralized or resentful. It also demonstrates your respect for them.

ETIQUETTE FOR DEVELOPING WORK RELATIONSHIPS

Purpose: *Use this job aid to review the rules of business etiquette you can use to enhance your professional relationships.*

You can use good workplace etiquette to build healthy relationships with colleagues, managers, clients, and others you interact with at work.

Being polite and cooperative

- Be polite in all situations, to people at all levels of the organization
- Always say "please" when making requests
- Always thank people when they've fulfilled your request or done something for you
- Always call people by their names – not nicknames or informal terms
- When dealing with introductions
    - introduce the more senior person first – what this means is that the higher-ranking person should be introduced first; if two persons are at the same rank, the older person should be introduced first
    - introduce people using first and last names
    - use small talk, like asking how the person is

  - ask people to remind you of their names if you forget them
- Celebrate colleagues' birthdays and special occasions
- Avoid turfism by cooperating with others and sharing your knowledge
- When others ask for your help, give them your full attention
- When you go to others for help, let them help when it's convenient for them, and don't pressure them unless your need for assistance is urgent

Keeping conversation professional

- Don't say things that could hurt or offend others; for example, avoid telling offensive jokes or mentioning offensive stereotypes
- Avoid subjects that are likely to provoke strong reactions
- Try not to let your personal problems affect your interactions with others at work

Showing respect

- Keep your physical interactions with others appropriate for the business environment
- Announce yourself before entering someone's office or cubicle
- Keep your noise levels down at work
- If you need to have personal conversations, do so in a private place instead of disrupting coworkers
- Criticize others only when it's necessary
- When you criticize others, do so sensitively and in private, and incorporate the criticism with relevant praise

Question

Wayne, a copywriter, is working on a new marketing campaign with Carlos, a senior graphic designer. Wayne is new to the company and is trying to build a good working relationship with Carlos.

How can Wayne enhance his relationship with Carlos?

Options:

1. Come up with a nickname for Carlos
2. Avoid making jokes or statements that draw on stereotypes
3. Excuse himself when they're working together and he needs to answer a personal call
4. Organize a special lunch for Carlos's birthday
5. Walk straight into Carlos's office when he needs help with visual concepts

Answer

Option 1: This option is incorrect. In a work context, calling someone by a nickname is unprofessional and may be considered impolite. Instead, Wayne should call Carlos by his name.

Option 2: This option is correct. Wayne can help keep his conversations with Carlos professional by avoiding potentially offensive jokes and topics.

Option 3: This is a correct option. Wayne can show Carlos respect by taking his personal calls in private, rather than in front of Carlos.

Option 4: This option is correct. Wayne can help develop his work relationship with Carlos by celebrating a special occasion like Carlos's birthday.

Option 5: This is an incorrect option. Walking into a colleague's office without announcing yourself is disrespectful. Wayne should respect Carlos's personal space by knocking on the door first.

3. SUMMARY

Following good business etiquette can help you build healthy professional relationships at work. One basic guideline is always to be polite and cooperative, regardless of who you're speaking to.

You should aim to keep conversations professional – taking care not to offend others and trying not to let personal problems negatively affect your workplace demeanor. It's also essential to show others respect. This involves avoiding any inappropriate physical interaction, respecting other people's personal space, and only delivering criticism in ways that are constructive, sensitive, and respectful.

BUSINESS ETIQUETTE CHECKLIST

Purpose: *Use this follow-on activity to assess how well you follow the basic rules of business etiquette and to find out how you can improve.*

Instructions for use: To use this tool, print the document or recreate the tables in a word processing or spreadsheet application and use it to complete the activity. Answer the questions with either "Yes" or "No." Then pick out instances where you answered "No" and consider how you could improve in these areas.

Being polite and cooperative	
Question	**Yes or no?**
Are you polite to colleagues and individuals at all levels of your organization?	
Do you say "please" and "thank you?"	
Do you call people by their real names instead of nicknames?	
Do you introduce higher-ranking people first? Or if both persons are at the same rank, do you introduce the older person first?	
Do you use first and last names when introducing people?	
Do you make small talk when meeting or intro-	

ducing people?	
Do you ask for a reminder of someone's name when you forget it?	
Do you celebrate birthdays and special occasions with others?	
Do you avoid turfism by cooperating with others and sharing your knowledge?	
When others seek your help, do you give them your full attention?	
When you go to others for help, do you allow them to help at a time that's convenient for them?	

Keeping conversation professional

Question	Yes or no?
Do you avoid saying things that could possibly offend or hurt others?	
Do you avoid subjects that could provoke strong reactions?	
Do you avoid letting personal problems affect your work interactions?	

Showing respect

Question	Yes or no?
Do you keep your physical interactions with others appropriate for a business environment?	
Do you announce yourself before entering someone's office or cubicle?	
Do you keep your noise levels down at work?	

Do you leave your place of work to have personal conversations in a private place?	
Do you criticize others only when it's necessary?	
When you criticize others, do you do so sensitively, in private, and together with relevant praise?	

DEFUSING CONFLICTS PROFESSIONALLY

After completing this topic, you should be able to recognize the guidelines for defusing conflicts professionally.

1. BENEFITS OF RESOLVING CONFLICT

To build strong professional relationships, you need to make a good first impression and follow proper business etiquette to continue building on this over time. You'll also need to manage any challenging situations or conflicts that arise in an appropriate way. In the workplace, conflicts may occur due to miscommunication, personal differences among coworkers, and disagreements about specific work-related issues.

It's important to take conflict in the workplace seriously. A conflict is more than just a simple disagreement. It's when the people involved perceive a threat to their needs or interests.

In conflict situations, this perceived threat is what tends to cause people to react instinctively or defensively, rather than considering problems objectively.

If conflict isn't resolved, differing perceptions can quickly turn into personal dislike. This can have a negative effect on teamwork and on morale. Conversely, the benefits of resolving conflict effectively include better understanding, strengthened group unity, and improved self-awareness.

See each benefit of resolving conflict effectively for more information about it.

Better understanding

In the process of resolving the conflict, you'll become more aware of why the situation occurred. You'll also develop a better understanding of the other person's needs and goals, making it easier to avoid further conflicts in the future.

Strengthened group unity

The process of successfully resolving conflict can help unify the members of a team, encouraging them to work together to achieve their goals and increasing mutual respect. Resolving conflict helps strengthen group unity as it helps colleagues overcome any issues that have developed. Then team members can work together, without emotion or disagreements preventing effective work being done.

Improved self-awareness

Working on resolving a conflict can help you become more aware of your own needs and interests. This can help you clarify your goals so you can focus on achieving them.

2. ETIQUETTE FOR RESOLVING CONFLICTS

When you're part of a conflict in the workplace, no matter who's to blame, you should always try to resolve it. You can resolve conflicts by following four rules of etiquette: be the first to make the move, choose the right time to approach the other person, be conciliatory, and take responsibility for how you've behaved.

When you have a conflict with someone, it's always good to be the first to attempt to resolve it. In a conflict situation, the other person might actively avoid you as a result of feeling uncomfortable and not knowing how to deal with the conflict. In this case, it's best to confront the conflict by approaching the person directly.

It's likely this person will appreciate you making the first move and so will be more open to finding a resolution.

However, it's important to choose the right time to address a conflict. You can approach the other person in private, and as soon as possible after the conflict occurs, to organize a sit-down meeting.

See each guideline for approaching someone for more information about it.

Approach in private

You can approach the other person in private to avoid embarrassment. For example, you could approach the person quietly in her office or when she is alone in a common area.

Approach as soon as possible

It's easy to avoid conflict and pretend it's not happening, but this won't solve anything. You need to approach the person as soon as the conflict arises or as soon as you become aware of it. It's best to deal with a conflict as early as possible to stop it from getting any worse.

Organize a meeting

When you approach the other person, you should explain that you think there's conflict between the two of you, and politely ask if it would be possible to discuss it in a meeting. Don't start by accusing the other person of wrongdoing.

Try to meet at a calm time of day that suits you both. For example, a meeting after lunch might be more constructive than one first thing in the morning when you're still trying to organize the day.

When you meet with a person to discuss a conflict, make sure you're conciliatory, and avoid showing any anger. Heated discussions can make a conflict worse. If you act calmly, it will encourage the other person to respond calmly too. Remaining conciliatory will help both parties stay objective and logical.

A final guideline for resolving conflict is that you should always take some of the responsibility. Conflicts are very rarely caused just by one party.

You should apologize for any of your actions that you think may have exacerbated the conflict. This doesn't mean you're taking responsibility for the whole conflict; you're just taking responsibility for your part in it.

For example, if you think you may have reacted unnecessarily to something the other person said, you can admit this and apologize for it. This may encourage the other person to apologize in return, and will help you work together to overcome the conflict.

RESOLVING CONFLICT

Purpose: *Use this job aid to review the guidelines for resolving conflicts in the workplace.*

There are four basic guidelines to resolve conflicts in the workplace.

1. Be the first to make a move

You should approach the other person first to try and resolve a conflict. If the person hasn't approached you, it may be because that person feels too awkward and doesn't know how to handle the situation.

2. Choose the right time to approach

You should make sure you approach the other person in private and at an appropriate time, but as soon as possible after the conflict arises. You should politely request a proper meeting at a calm time of day – for example, in the afternoon rather than first thing in the morning.

3. Be conciliatory and remain calm

When you discuss a conflict with someone, you should remain conciliatory and speak calmly. If you express frustration and anger, or make accusations, it's likely to make the situation worse. It's important to remain objective.

4. Take responsibility for your part

You should take responsibility for your part in creating a conflict. Ongoing conflicts are rarely caused by just one person. By apologizing for your role in the conflict, you'll encourage the other person to apologize also. Then you can work together to overcome the conflict.

Edith and Kyle are work colleagues. Edith has become aware of an ongoing conflict between Kyle and herself. She feels that Kyle intentionally finds flaws with all her ideas, especially in meetings. As a result, Edith has developed a habit of talking over Kyle, interrupting him and challenging him in meetings. Edith decides they need to resolve the conflict. She approaches Kyle when he's alone, and asks politely if they could meet toward the end of the day.

Follow along as Edith and Kyle meet to discuss the conflict between them.

Edith: Hi Kyle. Thanks for taking the time to meet with me.

Kyle: Not a problem. I'm actually quite glad you suggested a meeting.

Edith: Oh good. Well…as you're probably aware, there seems to be a conflict between us. I've noticed it especially during meetings. Do you agree there's a problem?

Kyle: Yes I do.

Edith: I'm aware I've recently started to interrupt and challenge you unnecessarily during meetings. I'd like to apologize for this.

Kyle: Thanks, Edith. I'm sorry for interrupting you too. I really don't mean to do it on purpose. It's something I need to work on.

Edith: OK, thanks. Sometimes it feels like you object to my ideas before even hearing what they are. I know I have less experience than you and could use some help with my proposals, but is there a reason why you tend to dismiss them so fast?

Kyle: Oh I didn't realize I did. I'm sorry if I came across that way. If you need some help with your ideas, would you consider letting me go over them with you? And meanwhile, I'll work on being more open to new ways of doing things.

Edith: That sounds great Kyle – I'd really appreciate your help.

Edith succeeds in resolving the conflict with Kyle by taking various steps. She decides to take action and is the first to make a move. She also acts early, before the conflict can spiral out of control.

Edith remains calm and conciliatory throughout the conversation. She doesn't vent her feelings of frustration or anger, and doesn't make any accusations.

By apologizing for her role in the conflict, Edith also encourages Kyle to apologize. Both Edith and Kyle can now work together to resolve the conflict, strengthening their professional relationship in the process.

Question

Holly has become aware of a conflict between a colleague, Matt, and herself. Holly feels that Matt always finds fault with her work and never encourages her. As a result, she's started being rude to Matt.

What can Holly do to help resolve the conflict?

Options:

1. Approach Matt when there are people around to mediate
2. Ask Matt politely if they could meet later in the day to discuss the conflict
3. Apologize for being rude to Matt
4. Be the first to admit to the conflict and approach Matt about it
5. Talk to Matt calmly and avoid making any accusations
6. Honestly express her anger and frustration to Matt

Answer

Option 1: *This is an incorrect option. You must approach someone about a conflict in private, rather than when other people are around.*

Option 2: *This is a correct option. To resolve a conflict, you can re-*

quest a proper meeting at a calm time of day. Many people are calmer toward the end of the day than early in the morning.

Option 3: This option is correct. To help resolve a conflict, you must always take responsibility for your part in it. By apologizing, you'll encourage the other person to apologize and take responsibility too.

Option 4: This is a correct option. You ought to deal with a conflict sooner rather than later, to prevent it from becoming worse. Be the first to make a move – the other person may feel too uncomfortable to do so.

Option 5: This option is correct. When meeting with someone to resolve a conflict, it's important to be conciliatory and to remain calm. This makes it possible for both parties to work together to overcome the conflict.

Option 6: This option is incorrect. When discussing a conflict with someone, you should be conciliatory and speak calmly. If you show anger or frustration, it could make the conflict worse.

3. SUMMARY

It's important to resolve conflicts in the workplace so they don't have a negative impact on your ability to work with others. Benefits of resolving conflicts effectively are that you'll gain a better understanding of other people's needs and goals, as well as of your own, and strengthen teamwork.

You can help resolve a conflict by following four rules of etiquette – be the first person to address the conflict, choose an appropriate time to approach the other person, remain conciliatory and calm, and take responsibility for your part in creating the conflict.

PRACTICE: BUILDING OFFICE RELATIONSHIPS

After completing this topic, you should be able to build office relation-ships using etiquette.

1. USING ETIQUETTE TO BUILD RELATIONSHIPS

A good work environment is one where people have healthy relationships. These relationships contribute to good productivity, teamwork, and success. When building such relationships, you need to follow essential rules of business etiquette.

In this topic, you'll get to practice applying the rules of etiquette, which require you to make a good first impression, be polite and cooperative, keep conversation professional, and show respect.

2. SUMMARY

You can help build good professional relationships by practicing proper business etiquette, which includes making a good first impression, being polite and cooperative, keeping conversation professional, and showing respect. In turn, this helps create a healthy and productive work environment.